UNDERSTANDIN
PSYCHOLOGY
BARBARA WOODS

UNDERSTANDING
PSYCHOLOGY
BARBARA WOODS

Hodder & Stoughton

A MEMBER OF THE HODDER HEADLINE GROUP

Orders: please contact Bookpoint Ltd, 130 Milton Park, Abingdon, Oxon OX14 4SB. Telephone: (44) 01235 827720. Fax: (44) 01235 400454. Lines are open from 9.00–6.00, Monday to Saturday, with a 24 hour message answering service. Email address: orders@bookpoint.co.uk

British Library Cataloguing in Publication Data
A catalogue record for this title is available from the British Library

ISBN 0 340 85648 3

First Published 2002

Impression number   10 9 8 7 6 5 4 3 2 1
Year   2008 2007 2006 2005 2004 2003 2002

Typeset by GreenGate Publishing Services, Tonbridge, Kent.

Printed in Spain for Hodder & Stoughton Educational, a division of Hodder Headline Plc, 338 Euston Road, London NW1 3BH by Graphycems.

To Jas, who made me find out more,
and who would have loved the colour.

Contents

Introduction

Understanding Psychology provides an introduction to the work and ideas of psychologists. It covers topics such as attachment, memory, anti-social behaviour, gender and prejudice, and considers how they relate to contemporary society. It has been written to accompany the new AQA Specification for GCSE Psychology, so it refers directly to the Specification content.

Each chapter covers a topic on the Specification and ends with sample exam questions. Research and theories are evaluated and their application to everyday life discussed. Throughout the book there are small 'boxes' which relate to research methods and issues. These illustrate the types of questions asked in the exam and set them in the context of the material as it is being studied. The chapters on research methods will assist students in devising and conducting their practical exercise.

Key terms are given in bold type in order to highlight their importance, and a glossary at the back provides explanations for frequently used terms.

AQA provides a GCSE Psychology Specification, Teachers' Guide and Specimen Papers and Mark Schemes, all of which provide essential information for teachers of the Specification. For further reading, many of the textbooks written for Advanced level students provide suitable material, and AQA publishes a list of books in their Teachers' Guide.

My aim has been to provide a textbook which is suitable for a wide range of abilities and yet includes sufficient information to achieve an A grade. Whether you use *Understanding Psychology* as a textbook or out of general interest, my hope is that you will find it enjoyable and stimulating.

Barbara Woods

Acknowledgements

My thanks to all those who have helped produce *Understanding Psychology*, in particular Emma Woolf for her gentle persistence, and Katie Chester at GreenGate, who has worked wonders. Thanks also to Mike Stanley of AQA for valuable feedback and to Tim Gregson-Williams who has negotiated the hurdles for me.

The author and publishers would like to thank the following for permission to use photographs:

Action Plus, Figure 3.7; Angela Hampton Family Life Pictures, Figures 7.1 and 7.3; Anti-Discrimination Commission, Queensland, Figure 2.2; Associated Press, Figure 8.1; Albert Bandura/Stanford University, Figure 9.2; John Callahan/Tony Stone Images, Figure 12.3; Les Editions Albert René, Figure 1.3; Ric Ergenbright/Corbis, Figure 1.4; Pascal Goatgheluck/ Science Photo Library, Figure 11.3; Harvard University Archives, Figure 10.8; J Allan Cash, Figure 1.1; Joyce Robertson/Concord Video and Film Council, Figure 4.2; Anthea CF King/Collections, Figure 8.2; The Kobal Collection, Figures 1.2 and 9.1; Life File/Nicola Sutton, Figure 9.5; © 1999 Lee Nolan/Hammond Productions, Figure 6.3; NYT Pictures, Figure 5.3; PA Photos, Figures 2.1, 9.3 and 12.6; PhotoDisc, Figure 10.7; Ulrike Preuss/Format, Figure 6.1; Range/Bettman/UPI, Figure 3.1; Redferns/David Redfern, Figure 1.5; Sally and Richard Greenhill, Figures 2.3, 4.1, 4.3, 5.1 and 8.4; Science Photo Library, Figure 11.4; Richard Sellers/Sportsphoto, Figure 9.4; Bob Witkowski/Corbis, Figure 12.3; Figure 6.2 Copyright © 2001 by Universal Studios, Inc. Courtesy of Universal Studios Publishing Rights, A Division of Universal Studios Licensing, Inc. All rights reserved.

While every effort has been made to trace copyright holders, this has not been possible in all cases; any omissions brought to our attention will be remedied in future printings.

Forming Impressions of Other People

Have you ever met someone for the first time and taken a dislike to them but then, as you get to know them better, your dislike evaporates? We are usually very quick to form impressions of people, often based on very little information. Psychologists have investigated the basis on which these impressions are formed, how accurate they are and what the implications might be for the way we interact with people. This is the focus of this chapter.

IMPRESSION FORMATION

We form impressions of others constantly and rapidly, but to do so we need to take 'short cuts'. From very little information we generate an impression of other people which may be biased or distorted. Some of these short cuts are described below.

CENTRAL AND PERIPHERAL TRAITS

Research has suggested that some information about people is more important than other information. Solomon Asch (1946) called this important information **central traits** and he showed how they influence the impression we form of others. One central trait is how 'warm' or 'cold' a person is. Asch gave two groups of participants an identical list of personality traits which he said described someone. The traits were:

intelligent skilful industrious _____ determined practical cautious

The difference between them was that one group saw 'warm' as the trait in the blank space, and the other group saw 'cold'. They were then given a list of additional traits (such as generous, wise, happy, good-natured, reliable) and asked to choose which of them this person would have. The results are shown in Table 1.1 on the next page. Participants reading the 'warm' list gave more positive additional characteristics than those reading the 'cold' list. In other words, participants' impressions of the person were biased by whether the person was described as warm or cold.

In another study Asch substituted the traits 'polite' or 'blunt' for the 'warm' or 'cold' traits. He found that these new traits had less impact on participants' impressions of the imaginary person, because they chose the additional traits in more similar percentages for both 'polite' and 'blunt'. These results have been compiled in Table 1.1 below. Asch concluded from these results that certain traits are central to the impression we have of others because they influence our perception of other, peripheral, traits.

Additonal traits	Traits inserted into description					
	Warm	or	Cold	Polite	or	Blunt
Generous	91%		8%	56%		58%
Humorous	77%		13%	71%		48%
Altruistic	69%		18%	29%		46%

Table 1.1 *Percentage of participants assigning additional traits to an imaginary person*

INTERPRETING RESULTS
Describe the results of Asch's study which are given in Table 1.1.

This study has been criticised because it requires participants to form an impression of a person who is imaginary. Nevertheless, Harold Kelley (1950) showed that warm/cold does affect our impression of others in real life. He gave students information on a new teacher which included the words either 'rather warm' or 'rather cold'. After they had all been in the same class with this new teacher, Kelley found that students reading the 'warm' information rated the teacher more highly (and interacted more with him) than those reading 'cold'. This supports the idea that warm/cold are examples of central traits, because on the basis of one word participants perceived the same person differently, and behaved differently towards him.

M. Rosenberg (1968) argued that it was the distinctiveness of the information which created the effect Asch found, because the warm/cold trait was a social one but all the other traits were intellectual ones. If someone is already described as helpful then warm does not add much more information. Rosenberg proposed that there are two major dimensions which underlie our assessment of others. One is the social/interpersonal dimension (which applies to warm/cold) and the other is the intellectual/competence dimension (which applies to intellectual abilities). Central traits are any traits which relate to either of these dimensions.

PRIMACY AND RECENCY EFFECTS

Imagine a new student joins your class. She seems pleasant and outgoing but after a couple of weeks she starts to demand a lot of the teacher's time. If someone asked you what you thought of her, you would probably say something like 'She seems OK'. That is, your first impression (which was pleasant) was stronger than the more recent one (unpleasant). The evidence that first impressions are more powerful than later ones is very strong, and this is called the **primacy effect**. We will look at the primacy effect before considering the circumstances in which the most recent information is the more powerful (called the **recency effect**).

THE PRIMACY EFFECT

A. Luchins (1957) tested primacy and recency by giving information about an imaginary person called Jim to four groups of participants. The information was in two parts: one part described Jim as outgoing, the other as shy. Each group read a different version of this information: one read a description in which Jim was outgoing but was then described as shy, a second group read a description in which he was shy but then became outgoing. The other two groups received only one piece of information, that he was either shy or outgoing. All participants then rated Jim for personality characteristics, including friendliness. Some of the results are given in Table 1.2.

Description	Percentage rating Jim as friendly
Outgoing description only	95%
Outgoing first – shy last	78%
Shy first – outgoing last	18%
Shy description only	3%

Table 1.2 *Percentage of participants rating Jim as friendly (Luchins, 1957)*

You can see that in the two groups receiving both types of information, what the participants read first determined their judgement of Jim's personality: this is evidence of the **primacy** effect. Participants also rated Jim more positively when the outgoing information was given first – he was thought to be more likeable and good-looking. This shows that the first impression biased participants' overall impression of Jim, giving him other positive characteristics.

Another study of the primacy effect involved participants watching a confederate solve difficult problems – he always got 15 of the 30 problems right. When he got most of the early problems right participants estimated his average was 20 out of 30 correct, but when he got most of the later problems right they estimated 12 out of 30 were correct. When asked the reasons for their judgements, those who saw the confederate's early right answers replied that the later wrong answers were due to tiredness or boredom, whereas if the early problems were wrong, his later success would be due to luck or guesswork.

Luchins found that the primacy effect is strongest when we are given information about someone we do not know. This could be because, as we know nothing about them, this first information is not modified by previous knowledge.

Figure 1.1 *First impressions count*

One criticism of primacy studies is that in everyday life our beliefs and experience with people provide us with information which may prevent the primacy effect occurring. As we will see shortly, **stereotyping** triggers our assumptions about people so we may not register that initial information.

THE RECENCY EFFECT

Under certain circumstances we do take more account of the last, the most recent, information we receive. This is known as the **recency effect** and it occurs when:

- we are careful not to make a judgement too early on
- there is a period of time between receiving the two lots of information
- the information is about people we already know
- the first information we receive is positive but it is followed by negative information. For example, if I describe a friend as sociable and reliable and having been drunk last night, then you are more likely to remember the last item, and your impression will be negative.

APPLICATION

If we do register our first impressions of a person, the primacy effect is important because we interpret subsequent information in the light of these first impressions. Research has shown primacy and recency can have an effect on the impressions jurors form when listening to the testimonies of witnesses in court.

First impressions can jeopardise success in an interview if the candidate is nervous. Interviewers have no previous knowledge of the candidate and are vulnerable to the primacy effect. It is therefore important for interviewers to try to put candidates at ease, to make notes throughout the interview and to hold back from making judgements until the interview is completed.

IMPLICIT PERSONALITY THEORIES`

Implicit personality theories are our own ideas about which personality traits go together. Here we will look at the halo effect and personal constructs.

THE HALO EFFECT

This refers to the kind of information we generate about a person based on one known factor which is either positive or negative. In Luchins' (1957) work on primacy (p. 3) when Jim was described as outgoing he was also thought to be more likeable and good-looking.

The most vivid example of the **halo effect** comes from how we judge a physically attractive person. Karen Dion (1972) found that attractive people in photographs were thought to be more sensitive, kind and interesting than less attractive people. Other research shows that attractive people are treated more leniently – whether they are writing poor essays or being tried in court.

Figure 1.2 *The attractiveness of this woman will affect the judgements that others make of her*

H. Harari and J. McDavid (1973) investigated the extent to which our names affect other people's assumptions about us. They asked experienced teachers to mark work written by 11-year-olds with a name attached. Some of the work, although identical, was given two different names. The teachers marked work written by a child with an attractive name (such as David or Karen) more highly than the same work written by a Hubert or Bertha. The results support the halo effect, because the attractive name led teachers to judge the work as better.

However, some participants may have responded to the **demand characteristics** (see p. 158) of the research. For example, if the teachers who were marking students' work recognised the work as identical but the names as different, they may have thought that they were expected to make different judgements as to the quality of the work. The only clue they had was the name, so they consciously gave different ratings in accordance with the names.

PERSONAL CONSTRUCTS

George Kelly (1955) proposed that through experience we develop our own theories about what people are like. He called these theories **personal constructs**, and each construct comprises a pair of opposite words, for example one person might have the construct 'friendly – unfriendly', but another's might be 'friendly – shy'. This shows that 'friendly' has a different meaning for each of these people.

Kelly maintained that these constructs represent the way we view the world, particularly the way we view other people and their behaviour. One person may have the friendly – shy construct and another have no construct related to these characteristics: it depends on what is important to them. Our personal constructs therefore shape our impressions of others.

- We use our personal constructs to organise information about our social world: we perceive others, and their behaviour, through our constructs. Imagine two people who meet the same person for the first time – she is very quiet. The individual with the friendly – shy construct sees this quiet woman as shy. But the other person has interesting – boring as one of his constructs, so he sees the quiet woman as boring. They perceive the same woman in a different way, indeed they will view most aspects of their social experiences in a different way: they construct their own social reality.
- We test our personal constructs (our theories of what the world is like) against what we see or experience. Our concern is not for objective truth but that our experiences fit our personal construction of the world. We are constantly checking these constructs against our experiences and may adapt them where necessary to fit new information.

Personal construct theory explains why each of us sees people in a different way, but because they are so personal we cannot make any general rules or predictions about how people will perceive others. Critics also say it stresses the individual's cognitive experience and largely ignores the effect others have on our behaviour (see Chapter 3, Social Influence), and the effect of the situation we are in.

APPLICATION

Much of the research in this field fails to reflect how we form impressions of other people in our everyday life. Participants are asked to form an impression of someone based on a verbal description or very little information, which is not the same as actually meeting someone, where we can gain impressions of them through all our senses.

The halo effect appears to happen when an individual has a particular feature which attracts attention and little else is known about the person. In everyday life we have more information about people, nevertheless this does have implications for the judgements we make about strangers, for example in interviews or as part of a jury. If people who are in these situations know they are likely to make biased judgements because of the halo effect or personal constructs, they can make an effort to counter this bias.

STEREOTYPING

A stereotype is a rigid, generalised and simplified set of ideas that we have about others. It can be applied to anyone we have identified as a member of a particular social group. We may identify them on the basis of visible cues, such as race, gender, physical shape or clothing, or less visible information such as job, sexual orientation or religion. By **stereotyping** we infer the person has a whole range of characteristics and abilities which we assume all members of that group have. Examples of commonly held stereotypes are that black people are good athletes, women are dependent, bank managers are cautious.

'That's the end of   'Rather'.
the season for
him, eh, what?'

'I say old chap,   'Let's not get
was that you   worked up. It's only
stamping on my   a game and all that
face, eh what?'   sort of thing'.

Figure 1.3 *These stereotypes about the English come from a French book*

THE CONTENTS OF STEREOTYPES

Students in America were asked for their stereotypes of ethnic groups, and if more than 75 per cent agreed on a personality trait this was considered a part of the stereotype (D. Katz and K. Braly, 1933). However, similar research 20 or 30 years later showed that some of these stereotypes had changed and that students were much more uncomfortable about being asked to make these kinds of generalisations.

In research which was designed to avoid obvious questions about stereotypes, G. Razran (1950) asked participants to rate pictures of girls on a range of psychological characteristics. Later they were asked to rate the same pictures but the girl was identified with a name which sounded either Irish, Italian or Jewish. Razran compared the original ratings with those linked to ethnicity, and found differences. For instance, when girls were given Jewish-sounding names they were rated higher on intelligence and ambition but lower on niceness. The conclusions seem to be that participants' judgements of the photographs were affected by their stereotype of a particular ethnic group.

Examples of gender stereotypes are included in Chapter 6, Sex and Gender on p. 66.

SOCIAL CATEGORISATION

Henri Tajfel (1971) proposed that stereotyping is based on a normal cognitive process – the tendency to group things together. In doing so we tend to exaggerate:

- the differences between groups
- the similarities of things in the same group.

We categorise people in the same way. We see the group to which we belong (the ingroup) as being different from the others (the outgroup), and members of the same group as being more similar than they are. We will look at these points in more detail below.

DIFFERENCES BETWEEN GROUPS

An important way in which we differentiate between groups is that we favour the ingroup over the outgroup. In a series of experiments, Tajfel and his colleagues (1971) aimed to show how easily people will discriminate against members of the outgroup.

Participants were 14- and 15-year-old boys. They were assigned to groups by the toss of a coin, so it was clear that their membership of a particular group was due completely to chance. They were told that the other participants were put into groups according to this chance method. As part of the research they were told that they could award points to their own group and the other group. These points were paired on a list, so for example if a boy gave 9 points to his own group the other group automatically received 11 points. They had to choose how to award these 'pairs' of points and were told they could redeem them for money at the end of the experiment.

Results showed that participants chose the pairings which created the biggest difference in points between their own and the other group (for example 7 for us, 1 for them). They did this even though a different choice would have gained them more points (for example 19 for us, 25 for them). The results therefore support Tajfel's prediction, that people will discriminate against members of an outgroup even when there is no prior prejudice or even proof that the other group exists.

SIMILARITIES WITHIN GROUPS

The other effect of social categorisation is that we tend to see members of outgroups as more similar than they really are, which is reflected in everyday comments such as 'they're all the same, these youngsters' or 'those Japanese all look alike to me' (see Figure 1.4). This is called **outgroup homogeneity** and it is the basis for the stereotype, the simplified set of ideas we have about other groups.

THE EFFECTS OF STEREOTYPING

Stereotyping is a way of organising and remembering information about people in a simple, generalised way. It reduces the amount of cognitive effort we need to make, but it also influences the way we perceive others because it:

- directs our attention to a particular feature of the individual (thus triggering the relevant stereotype)
- directs us to look for characteristics consistent with the stereotype (thus confirming the stereotype)

Figure 1.4 *Are members of the same group as alike as we tend to think?*

- tends to discount information which is inconsistent or exceptional (so the opportunity to break the stereotype is lost)
- helps us to interpret ambiguous information so it fits with the stereotype.

This is demonstrated in a study by M. Snyder and S. Uranowitz (1978) where participants were given a description of an imaginary person, including information that she never had a steady boyfriend in high school and that she went out on dates. Afterwards participants were given additional information: some were told she married, others were told she adopted a lesbian lifestyle. Results showed that participants later recalled more of the original information which conformed to their stereotype: those who were told she got married remembered her dates, those who thought she was lesbian remembered she never had a steady boyfriend.

This research shows that stereotypes distort the impressions we have of other people, leading us to view them as typical members of a group instead of responding to them as individuals. Michael Hogg and Dominic Abrams (1988) studied the effect of interest and motivation on social judgements and stereotyping. They found that when participants were told they would be working with someone from another group, they made more effort to find out about them. This suggests that increasing motivation to find out about others may reduce stereotyping.

How does stereotyping lead to positive or negative evaluations? The research by Tajfel (see p.8) highlighted the tendency to exaggerate differences between groups, favouring our own group in contrast to others. This preference for ingroup members has been demonstrated in many other experiments, and results show that we think our group is more attractive, intelligent, able and so on. When our group fails it is

Figure 1.5 *Evelyn Glennie is a world-famous percussionist. She is deaf. Does she fit your stereotype of a deaf person?*

due to bad luck, when the other group fails it is because they are not very good. In other words the stereotype for our group is positive and for outgroups it is more negative.

Why do we do this? In their **social identity theory**, Henri Tajfel and John Turner (1986) argue that membership of our group is an important source of pride and self-esteem which we enhance by:

- increasing the status of the group to which we belong – the ingroup
- denigrating or belittling groups to which we do not belong – the outgroup.

The more we need to raise our self-esteem, the more we are likely to denigrate the outgroup, which explains why some people are more prejudiced than others. We are also more likely to exaggerate the differences when the boundaries between the groups are unclear or when there is conflict between them. However, critics argue that the evidence is based largely on experimental work, and that in real life we enhance our own group, but we are much less likely to denigrate others.

We have noted that according to social identity theory we favour our own group. Thus, we have a shared belief that members of our own group have more positive qualities than members of other groups, simply because they belong to our group. In other words we have a **stereotypical** view of fellow group members.

According to Michael Hogg and John Turner (1987), once we have defined ourselves as a member of a social category, we learn the stereotypic **norms** of that category, accept these norms for ourselves and so feel we belong to the group. Hogg and Turner make the distinction between:

- **stereotypes** – which are descriptions and beliefs about people, and
- **norms** – which tell us how to behave and what is acceptable.

The stereotype for our group includes what people in our group believe about people in other groups. Accepting these stereotypes and acting in accordance with them (in other words discriminating) is a way of defining ourselves as a member of the group. This point is explored in terms of conformity in Chapter 3 (p.27).

In this discussion of stereotyping we have seen how social categorisation leads to stereotyping and positive or negative attitudes to others on the basis of the group they belong to. Stereotyping is related to our needs for self-esteem and belonging, but also, according to Tajfel (1981), it serves three functions in society, namely to:

- explain the causes of social problems, as happens in **scapegoating**
- justify discriminating against members of other groups
- justify treating others differently.

These are topics which are examined under Prejudice and Discrimination in Chapter 2.

EVALUATION AND APPLICATION

There are several criticisms of the material we have covered. These include:

- Research using artifically created groups does not reflect real life, where member-ship of a group has meaning to individuals, but where we also belong to many, overlapping groups. Imagine someone who is female, black and British. How will she view someone who is male, black and British or someone who is female, black and French?
- Investigations of the contents of stereotypes have focused on what is 'typical' or 'general'. Perhaps it is this very emphasis which has encouraged participants to gen-eralise their judgements. Related to this is the evidence that people are more reluctant to generalise, so perhaps in the earlier research participants were simply more willing to conform to the instructions of the researcher.
- Participants may not tell the truth about their beliefs, giving socially desirable responses.

The work on stereotyping has raised awareness of its relationship to prejudice, and is one of the reasons why it received attention in the USA as part of efforts to integrate black Americans, as well as people from other cultures, into American society. Tajfel represents the European view, seeing stereotyping as a normal cognitive process. By understanding it in this way we are able to identify the source of both negative and positive evaluations and this should help to tackle the negative impact of these evaluations.

The tendency to distinguish between our own group and the outgroup has been used to motivate people. For example, in the workplace, forming groups or teams of workers seems to raise self-esteem and can increase the effort people put into their work. If the effort of each group can be measured, people may be motivated to work harder in order to prove the superiority of their own group. This occurs naturally between teams in a sporting context.

Sample Exam Questions

1   What is meant by

   a   primacy effect *(2 mark)*
   b   recency effect? *(2 marks)*

2   Explain the difference between central traits and peripheral traits.
   (3 marks)

3   Describe one study in which impression formation was investigated.
   (5 marks)

4   What is a stereotype?
   (2 marks)

5   Explain how a stereotype can lead to a negative evaluation.
   (3 marks)

6   Describe one way in which research on impression formation can be applied to everyday situations.
   (3 marks)

CHAPTER

2

Prejudice and Discrimination

Read the national newspapers or listen to conversations and you will come across examples of prejudice. People express negative attitudes towards others because they are of a different religion, a different culture, a different race. We make assumptions about others based on their sexual orientation, their age, their physical appearance, their lifestyle. Why do we do this? In particular, how is it that we can hold negative attitudes about people we have never met? This chapter presents some of the answers to these questions which psychology provides, and looks at ways in which prejudice and discrimination can be reduced.

PREJUDICE AND DISCRIMINATION

Prejudice can be defined as an attitude, which is usually negative, towards a particular group of people, based on characteristics which are assumed to be common to all

Figure 2.1 *Tanni Grey-Thompson won several medals at the Paralympics in 2000 and flying around the world has become part of her everyday life. She has needed a wheelchair since she was seven years old and describes it as her most important thing because it gives her independence. Recalling an incident when the check-in staff at an airport wanted her to leave her own chair and be pushed on board in one of the airport models, she describes her refusal. As the queue lengthened behind her she suggested that the check-in clerk tell all the other people to take off their shoes and socks to go on board. The clerk replied 'We can't do that, it's a personal liberty issue!'. 'Precisely', replied Tanni.*

members of the group. Although prejudice can be positive or negative, psychologists have been much more concerned with its negative aspects because of their damaging effects.

Discrimination is treating people unfavourably on the basis of their membership of a particular group. Discrimination is usually, but not always, the behaviour resulting from prejudice. Discrimination includes ignoring someone, keeping a distance, using an unfriendly tone of voice, showing preference to others over them, harassing or even attacking them.

The link between a prejudiced attitude and discrimination is not always direct. A well-known study of discrimination was conducted by R. LaPiere (1934) who travelled extensively in the USA with a young Chinese couple. This was at a time of considerable anti-Chinese feeling. In all their visits to hotels and restaurants they experienced discrimination only once.

However, after visiting these establishments, LaPiere wrote to them asking about their attitudes to Chinese people. More than 100 replied, and 90 per cent of these said they would not accept Chinese clients. These results can be taken as evidence that prejudice is not directly linked to discrimination, although you may be able to think of other reasons for LaPiere's results.

EXPLANATIONS OF PREJUDICE

The possible causes of prejudice can be at the individual, interpersonal or intergroup level of explanation: below we look at examples of each.

AN INDIVIDUAL LEVEL OF EXPLANATION – THE AUTHORITARIAN PERSONALITY

The notion that prejudice can be due to a personality type was proposed by Theodore Adorno and his colleagues (1950) in America. In research to find an explanation for the behaviour of Nazi soldiers in World War Two they interviewed and tested hundreds of people. He and his colleagues found a particular pattern of personality characteristics which they called the **authoritarian personality**. Those with an authoritarian personality tended to be:

- hostile to those who are of inferior status but obedient and servile to those of higher status
- fairly rigid in their opinions and beliefs
- intolerant of uncertainty or ambiguity
- conventional, upholding traditional values.

Adorno concluded that these characteristics make them likely to categorise people readily into 'us' and 'them' groups, seeing their own as superior. This research also indicated that those with an authoritarian personality were more likely to have had a very strict upbringing by critical and harsh parents. Adorno claimed that they experienced unconscious hostility towards their parents which they were unable to express towards them. This hostility was displaced on to safer targets, namely those who were weaker and so unable to hurt them.

There are several weaknesses in Adorno's explanation. His identification of parenting style does not appear to be widely applicable because not all prejudiced people had harsh parents, and some prejudiced people show few features of the authoritarian personality. Also, he only found a **correlation** between parenting style and the authoritarian personality.

The authoritarian personality also fails to explain why many people are prejudiced, nor does it explain why we are prejudiced against certain groups rather than others. It seems we need to take account of some aspects of our social setting to explain these points.

THE AUTHORITARIAN PERSONALITY IN EVERYDAY SITUATIONS

There is evidence for the pattern of attitudes and behaviours termed the authoritarian personality which suggests that although not common, it is quite a robust concept. Given this evidence, and the rigid nature of the views held, it would be very hard to change the views (and prejudices) of the authoritarian personality. As we shall see later, some people do appear to be very resistant to changing their prejudiced views, and this may be explained by the authoritarian personality.

THE INTERPERSONAL LEVEL OF EXPLANATION

At the interpersonal level, prejudice is seen as arising from within social groups. Here we will look at **social identity theory** and conformity to social norms.

SOCIAL IDENTITY THEORY

In Chapter 1 under Stereotyping (p. 8) we noted the ease with which we categorise people into our own group (the ingroup) and the other group (the outgroup). Henri Tajfel (1971) called this **social categorisation** and it is the first step in the stereotyping process. He argued that we accentuate the differences between our group and the outgroup.

As a result of work with John Turner, Tajfel proposed that the groups we are part of – our psychology class, football team, neighbourhood and so on – are an important source of pride and self-esteem (Tajfel and Turner, 1986). They give us our **social identity**: a sense of belonging in the social world. In order to increase our self-image we enhance the status of the groups to which we belong. For example, research shows that we think members of our own group are more attractive and intelligent than those in the outgroup. We also judge our group in circumstances where it is successful and tend to dismiss situations in which it does badly.

Critics argue that the evidence is based largely on experimental work, which is artificial. In real life we tend to enhance our own group but we do not necessarily denigrate others. So although we differentiate between the ingroup and the outgroup, we do not necessarily have negative feelings towards the outgroup. Nevertheless we do treat outgroup members differently, so we discriminate against them.

CONFORMITY TO SOCIAL NORMS

This explanation says that we are prejudiced because we are conforming to the norms of our group or society. As a result, the targets of prejudice can change if social norms change. For instance, during World War Two, American government propaganda shaped American attitudes to Japanese and Germans as negative, and towards

Understanding Psychology

Russians (who were allies) as positive – hardworking and so on. After the war, as the Americans and the Russians became enemies, the propaganda changed and the Russians were portrayed in a negative way – as cruel, for example. Research showed that American attitudes towards Russians became much more negative; it became acceptable, even proof of being a good American, to denigrate the Russians. This explanation for prejudice suggests that it is transient. Indeed, R. Minard (1952) showed that prejudice and discrimination towards a particular group may be evident in one setting but not in another. He studied black and white coal miners in West Virginia and found that there was integration below the ground (at work) but segregation above ground (in the wider social world). The fact that prejudice and discrimination varied like this suggests that one set of social norms operated below ground whilst the social norms operating above ground were those of the wider society in which these men lived.

INTERPERSONAL EXPLANATIONS IN EVERYDAY SITUATIONS

Social identity theory and conformity to social norms are explanations that emphasise the part which others play in influencing our attitudes and behaviour, particularly those who are part of our social group. We learn the contents of **stereotypes** and the norms of the group to which we belong from those around us. This explains why the contents of stereotypes and the targets of prejudice can change.

However, when our self-esteem is bound up in the groups we belong to, as social identity theory proposes, then it will be difficult to reduce prejudice. Nevertheless social identity theory explains why discrimination occurs.

Can the law reduce prejudice? Even when prejudice is illegal, social norms may condone or even encourage it. A cross-cultural study carried out in Holland and America looked at how racism is communicated between white people. Results indicated that in the wider society it was not acceptable to show racism, but within various subgroups (such as the family, in the workplace, amongst neighbours) racist talk and behaviour was acceptable. Conformity to social norms appears to be a powerful explanation for prejudice and discrimination.

Figure 2.2 *Advertisement indicating anti-discrimination laws*

THE INTERGROUP LEVEL OF EXPLANATION

At the intergroup level, prejudice has been explained as due to competition which exists between various groups in society. This may be political or economic competition, and is most intense when resources are limited. For instance, when jobs are scarce there may be an increase in prejudice towards minority groups, or when one group gains political power and uses it to benefit its own members at the expense of others. These types of circumstances can be explained by the idea of intergroup conflict or by scapegoating.

INTERGROUP CONFLICT

Muzafer Sherif argued that intergroup conflict occurs when two groups are in competition for scarce resources. This proposition was based on the results of a **field experiment** conducted by Sherif and his colleagues (1961). They observed the behaviour of 12-year-old boys who were attending a summer camp called The Robber's Cave. The 22 participants were not known to each other and all were white, psychologically well adjusted and from stable middle-class homes. They were randomly assigned to two groups but neither was aware of the other's existence.

RANDOMISATION
Randomisation is the process of ensuring that each member of the target population has an equal chance of being selected for one group or the other. To do this, Sherif and his colleagues could have written the name of each participant on a slip of paper, put the 22 slips in a box, stirred them about and then taken them out one at a time. The first 11 names could have formed one group, the rest the other, or the names could have been assigned alternately to each group.

For a few days, normal summer camp activities took place and both groups quickly established their own culture – naming themselves the 'Rattlers' and the 'Eagles' and developing group norms.

Then a series of intergroup contests were devised by the counsellors, the group winning the series getting a silver cup. In addition, situations were devised in which one group gained at the expense of the other, for example one group was delayed getting to a picnic and when they arrived the other group had eaten most of the food. Hostility quickly arose, and groups derided and attacked each other. Each group became more united, and the more aggressive boys became leaders.

The next stage in the study was to reduce prejudice by increasing social contact in a non-confrontational way, for instance they all ate together and went to see a film. However this was not effective, and it was not until the final stage (which is described on p. 20 under Reducing Conflict) that hostility was eliminated. Sherif concluded that competition increases both the cohesiveness within groups and their hostility towards other groups.

The Robber's Cave study has been criticised on the basis that the groups were artificial, as was the competition, and so they did not necessarily reflect real life. Nor should the results be generalised because the research used only 12-year-old white boys and excluded, for example, girls and adults.

SCAPEGOATING

According to this explanation there are always frustrations in life, and these can build up to unacceptable levels in some people, particularly if they are in difficult circumstances such as unemployment or poor housing. According to the **frustration–aggression hypothesis** (see p. 97) this frustration leads to anger and aggression which has to be released. Often this cannot be directed at the causes because they are many and complicated, and we may not even know what they are. Instead it is displaced onto groups which society considers to be acceptable targets for hostility and aggression. In other words, these groups are used as **scapegoats**; we blame them for our frustration and release our aggression against them.

There is evidence that those who feel most threatened during an economic recession show an increase in prejudice against particular groups. This was investigated by C. Hovland and R. Sears (1940), who amassed statistics relating to lynchings of black Americans in the US and failures in the cotton crop from 1880 to 1930. They found a **negative correlation** between these two variables – the number of lynchings increased as economic conditions deteriorated.

INTERGROUP EXPLANATIONS IN EVERYDAY SITUATIONS

The intergroup level explains why many people may be prejudiced (due to competition or frustration), and why they are prejudiced only towards certain groups (those they compete against or blame). There is certainly evidence for scapegoating – politicians may create scapegoats in order to redirect public frustration away from themselves. For instance, working mothers have been blamed for job shortages and juvenile crime, Adolf Hitler blamed Germany's economic problems on Jews.

One example of conflict between groups is in sport. Football teams, for instance, are pursuing the same goal – to win – so there should be considerable hostility between opposing players. However, this does not seem to be the case: many players are friends off the pitch, so competition for scarce resources does not in itself create prejudice and discrimination.

REDUCING PREJUDICE AND DISCRIMINATION

Prejudice (the negative attitude) and discrimination (the resultant behaviour) are damaging to a society, as well as being unjust, which is why psychologists have studied ways of reducing it. Below we consider some strategies for reducing prejudice and discrimination.

SOCIAL CONTACT

If prejudice and discrimination are based on lack of knowledge about members of others groups, increasing the contact between members of these groups should give people more information about others, and thus break down stereotypes. However, as Sherif found in The Robber's Cave study, it is not enough to simply bring people together (see p. 17). Minard's (1952) study of miners, which is described on page 16, also provides evidence. Despite social contact at work, the miners still discriminated in their social lives above ground.

In the 1970s Aronson noted that there had always been contact between black and white Americans, yet it had not reduced prejudice and discrimination. He argued that because whites saw black workers only doing menial jobs, contact merely reinforced their stereotypes and prejudice. Research shows that the more effective ways of reducing prejudice and discrimination through social contact are:

- When those experiencing prejudice and discrimination are of higher status than the discriminator (for example, those with better jobs or a higher level of education). Research suggests that when members of two groups are in contact, it is invariably the higher-status members who dominate – they tend to initiate things and be listened to by others, and their views are more likely to be followed. If the members of both groups are of equal status it is not enough to 'tip the balance' in favour of those experiencing discrimination.
- If the individuals who are in contact are seen as members of a group, and not as individuals. Prejudice towards the individual may be reduced, but is less likely to generalise to all members of that group.
- When there is social support for reducing prejudice and discrimination, such as laws making discrimination illegal, social norms of toleration and respect for others.

Figure 2.3 *Increasing contact may not be enough to reduce prejudice and discrimination*

CO-OPERATION

In The Robber's Cave study (see p. 17) Sherif found that hostility was finally eliminated when all the boys co-operated so as to achieve goals which could not be achieved unless both groups worked together. For instance, they pulled a truck back to camp in order to get there in time for lunch. After several tasks such as this, the intergroup hostility disappeared and indeed several boys became good friends with boys in the other group.

However, the success of this strategy is probably due to the superficial nature of the prejudice and discrimination which Sherif's study created. The conflict was artificial, as was the difference between the groups. When the groups worked together the boys would have seen the other white middle-class boys as similar, and they would have easily formed a new group with a common goal.

How easy is it to reduce conflict between groups with long standing prejudice and discrimination, whose differences are clearly visible and supported by social norms? When Elliot Aronson and his colleagues (1978) were called in by a Texas school to devise some ways of reducing prejudice between the white and black students, they devised the **jigsaw technique** to increase co-operation.

The jigsaw technique involved small groups of racially mixed students, each of whom had to work on a part of a lesson. In order for the whole class to cover all the material, the individuals in the groups worked together first, and then communicated their group work to the rest of the class. When Aronson evaluated the strategy he found increased co-operation, self-esteem and academic performance. He also noted more positive perceptions of those of the other racial group, which would suggest that stereotypes were breaking down.

However, this did not appear to be the case because these new perceptions were not generalised to every member of the racial group. These students saw each other as exceptions to the stereotypes, but the stereotypes themselves did not change very much. So although co-operation strategies can reduce prejudice, the individual may not generalise these new attitudes to others when they are in a different setting.

Other research has founded mixed benefits from the use of co-operation to reduce prejudice. This is illustrated in an American study which arranged for very prejudiced white and black people to work together on a series of joint tasks. Results showed that six months later 40 per cent of the participants were much less prejudiced, 40 per cent had not changed their attitudes and 20 per cent had become more prejudiced.

CREATING EMPATHY

If we experience the effects of prejudice and discrimination, we might try to change our attitudes. In an effort to do this with her class of nine-year-olds, Jane Elliott (1977) divided the children into two groups on the basis of their eye colour: blue-eyed and brown-eyed.

Then she told them that brown-eyed people were better and more intelligent than those with blue eyes, so they would be given extra privileges. The blue-eyed students wore collars to distinguish them, and had to wait until the end of the line and have less break time. The children started to behave according to these stereotypes: the brown-eyed became more dominant, produced better work and started to treat the blue-eyed children badly, whilst the blue-eyed became angry or depressed and their work deteriorated.

The next day she told them she had made a mistake and that blue-eyed people were superior: the patterns of prejudice and discrimination quickly reversed. On the third day she told them the truth, that there were no such differences but that she wanted them to feel what it was like to be judged on the basis of one, irrelevant, physical feature which they could not change.

This technique seemed to be effective in reducing prejudice, because when Elliott contacted these students at 18 years of age, she found that they were more tolerant of differences between groups and more opposed to prejudice than a control group comprised of a class who had not gone through the brown-eyed/blue-eyed experience.

PREJUDICE REDUCTION IN EVERYDAY SITUATIONS

The likelihood that these techniques will reduce prejudice in everyday life will vary for several reasons. For example:

- The success of Jane Elliott's work using empathy may have been due to the age of the children, whose stereotypes and attitudes were probably more flexible than those of adults. Creating empathy in people with prejudiced views may be more difficult to accomplish.
- The success of the jigsaw technique may have been due in part to the role of the teacher. The technique and the teacher are establishing a norm of mutual respect and co-operation, treating each student equally regardless of race. The ingroup was the class as a whole, but this did not reflect wider society. The social norms which support prejudice must also be tackled if efforts to reduce prejudice are to be generalised to a wider social context.
- It may not always be possible to ensure that people who are prejudiced only come into contact with higher-status members of a discriminated group.
- Even when these techniques fail in general terms, they may still be valuable in a restricted social setting such as a school or workplace. However, these too are competitive environments, and it is this aspect which may provide a basis for hostility.
- Variables which contribute to successful co-operation (such as a goal of equal value to both groups, or guaranteed success) may be difficult to control in an everyday setting. If the goal is not achieved, blame may fall on the members of the minority group, thus strengthening prejudice.

Sample Exam Questions

1 Describe one study in which the development of prejudice was investigated. Indicate in your answer the reason why the study was conducted, the method used, the results obtained and the conclusions drawn.
(5 marks)

2 a Outline Adorno's explanation for prejudice and discrimination.
  (3 marks)
  b Discuss how this relates to an everyday situation.
  (3 marks)

3 Discuss an interpersonal explanation for prejudice with reference to the work of Tajfel.
(5 marks)

4 Use your knowledge of psychology to describe one intergroup explanation of prejudice.
(5 marks)

5 a Identify one way that prejudice and discrimination may be reduced.
  (1 mark)
  b Use psychological evidence to describe how this might be put into effect.
  (4 marks)

6 Using your knowledge of psychology, discuss the likely success of attempts to reduce prejudice in everyday situations.
(5 marks)

Social Influence

Psychologists who have studied social influence want to find out how other people affect our behaviour. If you are doing a project in class, do you prefer to work alone or in a group? Have you ever laughed at a joke which was not funny, simply because everyone else did? At the other extreme, why will someone obey another person, even to the point of killing innocent people? Research suggests that the atrocities in Nazi Germany, Vietnam or Bosnia could have been performed by many of us. This chapter looks at some of the research which has tried to discover how and why other people influence our behaviour.

SOCIAL FACILITATION

When people are working side by side, they often perform better than if they are working alone. This was noted by Norman Triplett (1898) when he compared the times recorded by cyclists who were in training and found those cycling in pairs were faster than those training alone. Triplett concluded that this increase in performance was due to the fact that someone else was doing the same task alongside them.

An explanation for this could have been the competitive nature of the task, but Floyd Allport (1924) found that this effect occurs even when there is no apparent element of competition. He asked participants to do a variety of tasks, such as multi-plication sums or crossing out vowels in a newspaper article. The results showed that participants worked better when they could see others doing the same task than when they were working alone. Allport called this the **co-action effect**.

EXPERIMENTAL DESIGN
Allport's research used the repeated measures design, because his par-ticipants took part in both conditions of his experiment, doing the tasks alone and doing them alongside others. He could have used an inde-pendent measures design, in which half the participants worked alone and half worked in groups. Why do you think he chose the repeated measures design? See p. 156 to help you answer this question.

SOCIAL FACILITATION IN EVERYDAY LIFE

Social facilitation can be used to improve people's performance in a variety of settings, such as work (see Figure 3.1), school and sports. Social facilitation may explain the popularity of aerobics classes – people put more effort into their exercises when others are doing the same thing than when watching an exercise video alone at home. At school, if children are doing individual tasks (such as completing a science worksheet) they may put in more effort if they can work alongside other children at the same table.

Figure 3 .1 *According to the co-action effect, these typists working in 1929 were typing faster than if they had been working alone*

AUDIENCE EFFECTS

An individual's performance may also be affected when someone is watching – this is known as the **audience effect**. Research shows that an audience has one of two effects:

- participants doing an easy task perform better when there is an audience
- participants doing a difficult task perform worse when there is an audience.

For example, J. Michaels and colleagues (1982) assessed the ability of some pool players over several games and rated them as either above or below average, based on the percentage of shots that went into the pocket. The researchers then stood by the pool table as play was going on, to see if their presence had any effect. The results are shown in Table 3.1.

Standard of player	Change in accuracy of shots
Above average players	Increased from 71% to 80%
Below average players	Decreased from 36% to 25%

Table 3.1 *Changes in accuracy of shots by pool players when being watched by others (Michaels et al., 1982)*

The conclusions are that an audience improves the performance of well-learned skills but damages the performance of poorly learned skills. Robert Zajonc (1966) explains this effect as being due to the increased arousal caused by the presence of others. This arousal stimulates us, so that if we are doing something we are good at, we do it better. However, we are already aroused when we are doing a difficult task (such as one which is complicated or new), so the presence of others creates an overload of arousal and interferes with our ability to do the task.

AUDIENCE EFFECTS IN EVERYDAY LIFE

Improvements in performance have been noted in the employment setting. The **Hawthorne effect** refers to research on factory workers which showed that when they were observed, their productivity increased regardless of their work environment. Even when conditions were made worse, productivity increased. One of the explanations is that it was due to the audience effect – these workers knew they were being observed.

There are many other situations in which our level of competence must be judged by others, such as taking a driving test, a French oral exam or performing in sport. Robert Zajonc's explanation of why others can improve or damage our performance can help us prepare for these situations. Clearly we need to be competent in the task, but also if we practice performing it in front of others then there is less likelihood of arousal overload during the actual performance.

SOCIAL LOAFING

When people are working together in a group, each individual tends to reduce their own effort. This is known as the Ringelmann effect after Max Ringelmann (1913) measured the amount of effort men put into a tug-of-war task and found the greater the number of men that were pulling, the less effort each individual put in.

Bibb Latané used the term **social loafing** for this effect and has demonstrated it in a number of studies, for example Latané and his colleagues (1979) asked participants to shout and clap and make as much noise as they could, sometimes alone, sometimes with one other or else in a group of four or six. They wore headsets so they did not know how much noise the others were making: the researchers recorded the amount of noise each participant made.

The results showed that the larger the group, the less effort the individual made. The individual's output of sound, when working with five others, was reduced to about one-third of their output when alone. Latané and his colleagues concluded that people were making less effort in groups because others were contributing to the task.

SOCIAL LOAFING IN EVERYDAY LIFE

As we have seen in the earlier topics, work, education and sport settings provide opportunities for social loafing. To avoid social loafing effects in team sports, coaches are advised to provide feedback on performance to individuals as well as the whole team.

When students work together on group projects it is important that teachers can identify the effort put in by each member. They may, for example, ask each group member to assess the others. Target setting is now common in hospitals, schools and universities as well as in manufacturing and selling. Providing public information about what each individual or section should achieve is a way of identifying performance within a larger group.

It appears that social loafing is a predominantly Western phenomenon, related to our individualist culture. In collectivist cultures (see p.30) the opposite occurs, and this is called 'social striving'. Harry Triandis (1990) noted that in collectivist cultures individual goals are not as important as the goals of the whole group.

BYSTANDER BEHAVIOUR

Bystander behaviour is the term used for the way people act when there is an emergency. What makes, or stops, people from helping others? There are a few vivid examples of someone being murdered or a child abducted with no-one stepping in to help. This is explored in greater detail in Chapter 8, Pro-social Behaviour (see p. 86), but here we will focus on two experiments which demonstrate the effect that others might have on our behaviour in an emergency.

MORE BYSTANDERS, LESS HELP?

John Darley and Bibb Latané (1968) were interested to find out what people would do in an emergency which other people also knew about. They asked participants to discuss a topic with some other people who were close by. However, they were told this was to be through an intercom so as to reduce embarrassment during the discussion.

There were three conditions:

- the participant thought there was only one other person in the discussion
- the participant thought there were two others
- the participant thought there were five others in the discussion.

Early in the discussion one of the others casually mentioned that he sometimes had seizures and later in the discussion it appeared that he was having a seizure. How did participants respond? The researchers noted how many participants sought help within the first 4 minutes. The results are shown in Table 3.2.

Darley and Latané concluded that the more 'others' that are present, the less likely any one person is to help. They called this diffusion of responsibility: the more bystanders who might help, the less we take personal responsibility for action.

Number of others hearing seizure	Percentage going to help
Participant alone	85%
Participant and one other	62%
Participant and four others	35%

Table 3.2 *The percentage of participants seeking help and size of the group (Darley and Latané, 1968)*

IMITATING OTHERS

If someone else goes to help, does that encourage others to follow their example? The answer appears to be yes. A study by J. Bryan and M. Test (1967) took place at the side of a motorway. They arranged for a woman (a confederate) to stand beside a car with a flat tyre – this was the test condition. In the experimental condition a 'helping situation' was set up one-quarter of a mile before the car with the flat tyre. Here a woman was stood beside a car watching a man change the tyre; he provided the **model** for helping.

Results showed that of the many cars which passed during the experiment, more stopped to help when they had passed the 'helping situation' than when there was no helping situation. We can conclude that people are more likely to help others when they have seen someone else model helping behaviour.

BYSTANDER BEHAVIOUR IN EVERYDAY LIFE

These studies demonstrate circumstances which affect whether or not people help in an emergency, a topic which is explored in more depth in Chapter 8. It seems that awareness of research on bystander behaviour does make people more aware of the need to take action. Certainly, if someone offers help, they are taking personal responsibility and provide a model for other bystanders.

CONFORMITY

Although most of us like to feel that we make our own decisions, in reality we often adjust our actions or opinions so that they fit in with other people. **Conformity** is yielding to the perceived pressure of group members, even though no-one tells us to do so.

Muzafer Sherif (1935) tested conformity using the **autokinetic effect** – a visual illusion in which a stationary dot of light appears to move when shown in a very dark room. Participants were asked how far they thought the light moved and those who were alone when they saw the light gave estimates of between 2 and 25 cm. Then the participants viewed the light in groups of three over a series of trials, and each person estimated in public how far they thought the light moved. These estimates became closer and closer after each trial: a **group norm** emerged even though participants were not asked to do this. You can see the results in Figure 3.2 below.

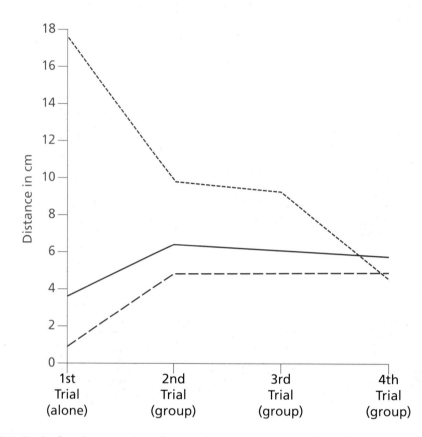

Figure 3.2 *Typical estimates given by participants individually and then within a group*

Afterwards, each participant saw the light alone and their estimate remained close to the group norm. Sherif concluded that this showed how easily group norms emerge and are then adhered to. Criticism came from Solomon Asch (1951) who argued that Sherif's participants were influenced by the group norm because they were not certain of the answer.

Test line   Comparison lines

Asch investigated conformity when there is no uncertainty, using groups of six to nine people. One was a participant, but the rest were confederates who had been told to give wrong answers on certain trials. Asch said he was testing visual perception and presented the group with lines of different lengths. Each person had to judge whether line A, B or C was the same length as the test line (see Figure 3.3).

Figure 3.3 *An example of the test line and the comparison lines in Asch's (1951) experiment*

The participant was one of the last to give his judgement (see Figure 3.4) and in control trials when participants were tested alone, there were very few wrong answers. But Asch found that when they became part of a group, 25 per cent of participants conformed to the rest of the group on most of the occasions when the group was wrong. Overall, 75 per cent of participants conformed to the wrong answer at least once. The average rate of conformity was 32 per cent.

Figure 3.4 *The only person who does not know what is going on is the participant – number 6. In these photographs he is giving his judgement after each of the five men before him have given an obviously wrong answer.*

When participants were interviewed afterwards, most said they knew they were giving the wrong answer but, for example, did not want to look a fool or upset the experiment. Asch concluded that people show a high level of conformity even in unambiguous situations because of the desire to fit in with the group.

FACTORS AFFECTING CONFORMITY

In further trials, Asch changed the procedure in order to investigate which factors influenced the level of conformity. His results and conclusions are given below:

- **Group size** – with one other person in the group conformity was 3 per cent, with two others it increased to 13 per cent and with three or more it was 32 per cent. So people are more likely to conform when in larger groups. Because conformity does not seem to increase in groups larger than four, this is considered the optimal group size.
- **Lack of unanimity** – when one other person in the group gave a different answer from the others, and therefore the group answer was not unanimous, conformity

dropped. This was true even if that person's answer was wrong, indicating that if one other disagrees, the individual is less likely to conform.

* **Anonymity** – when participants could write their answers down rather than announce them in public, conformity dropped. This suggests that individuals conform because they are concerned about what other people think of them.
* **Ambiguity** – when the lines were made more similar in length it was harder to judge the correct answer and conformity increased, reflecting Sherif's results. When we are uncertain, it seems we look to others for confirmation.
* **Cultural context** – later replications of Asch's work have generally not found similar levels of conformity, possibly because it took place when there was a strong anti-Communist/pro-American culture which encouraged people to conform to the social norms of the period. Others have found that in collectivist cultures (where the importance of one's family, religion or race is paramount) there seem to be higher levels of conformity than in individualist cultures (where independence is most valued).

M. Deutsch and H. Gerrard (1955) have proposed two types of social influence. When we are unsure about something, perhaps because it is ambiguous, we look to others for answers. This is **informational** social influence and it explains Sherif's results and the reason for greater conformity when line lengths were similar. **Normative** social influence occurs when we want approval and acceptance from others. This explains why there was greater conformity when there were more people, and why the social norms at the time were influential. We return to the influence of group norms later in this chapter (p. 34).

EVALUATION OF RESEARCH ON CONFORMITY

In an amended version of the original method, Asch used a group of participants and one confederate. It was he who gave the wrong answer, but the participants asked if he could see properly and started laughing – as did the researcher eventually! This illustrates how the lack of response by confederates in Asch's original studies emphasised the artifical nature of the situation to the participants.

Asch's conclusions were based on mean levels of conformity, but in fact there were wide variations. This suggests an equally interesting question – why are some people able to resist group pressure?

OBEDIENCE

Obedience means following the orders of someone who we perceive to be in authority. One of the most widely known psychological studies was carried out by Stanley Milgram (1963) who investigated how far people would go in obeying orders from someone else.

Each participant was a 'teacher' who was paired with a 'learner' (a confederate). A researcher took them into a room where the learner was strapped into a chair with electrodes attached to his arms (see Figure 3.5). The teacher and researcher then went into an adjoining room which contained a shock generator with a row of switches marked from 15 volts ('slight shock') to 375 volts ('danger: severe shock') right up to 450 volts.

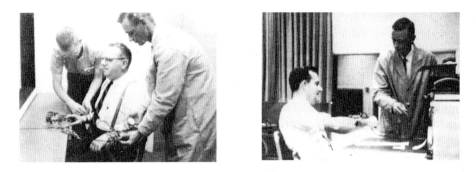

Figure 3. 5 *Milgram's 'learner' having the electrodes strapped on and the participant receiving a sample shock from the generator*

The machine did not actually deliver shocks, but the participant was given a 45-volt shock (apparently from the machine) in order to make the procedure convincing.

The participant was instructed to read out word pairs (such as 'blue–girl') for the learner to remember. The teacher was to give the learner an electric shock if he made a mistake or said nothing; if errors continued the shocks were to be increased. The learner started off quite well, but as he made more and more mistakes, the teacher had to increase the shocks. At 180 volts the learner shouted out that he could not stand the pain, at 300 volts he begged to be released, after 315 volts there was silence. Of course this was all artificial.

Before starting, Milgram showed this description of the study to psychiatrists for their comments. They predicted, as did Milgram, that around 2 per cent would shock to the highest level but the majority would refuse to continue at a very early stage. However, all participants shocked to 300 volts and 65 per cent of participants continued to 450 volts. Despite this, participants showed considerable distress during the experiment. Three had seizures, several challenged the experimenter and asked if the learner could be checked. The experimenter responded with verbal 'prods' such as 'although the shocks are painful there is no permanent damage so please go on' or 'you have no other choice, you must continue'. Afterwards all the participants were debriefed.

ETHICS – DEBRIEFING

Participants must be thoroughly debriefed at the end of the research, as detailed on p. 161. Milgram debriefed his participants by telling them what was really happening in the study. They were shown that the apparatus did not deliver shocks and were introduced to the learner so they could see that he was unharmed. They were assured that their own behaviour was normal. When Milgram followed up each participant several months later to ask their opinion of the research and whether they had experienced any problems, he noted that 74 per cent said they had learned something of personal importance from the experiment.

FACTORS AFFECTING OBEDIENCE

In variations of the basic procedure, Milgram identified a number of factors which affected obedience; his results and conclusions are shown below.

Obedience increases when:

- Orders are given by an authority figure – Milgram's experimenter wore a laboratory coat (a symbol of scientific expertise), but when dressed in everyday clothes obedience was very low. Leonard Bickman (1974) tested this in a real-life setting by having researchers give orders to pedestrians in New York. Researchers were dressed as either a guard, a milkman or wearing a sports coat and tie. Pedestrians were most likely to obey the 'guard', suggesting that an authority figure elicits higher levels of obedience.
- Orders are given in a prestigious setting – when Milgram's study was conducted in a run-down office in the city, roughly one-third fewer participants shocked to the maximum. This suggests that prestige increases obedience.
- There is less personal responsibility – when participants could instruct an assistant to press the switches, 95 per cent instructed to shock to 450 volts.

Obedience decreases when:

- Others disobey authority – when two other 'teachers' (who were confederates) refused to give the shock, obedience dropped to 10 per cent. Several participants said afterwards that they had not realised they could refuse to continue. This suggests that seeing a disobedient model reduces obedience.
- Proximity is greater – the closer participants were to the learner the lower the shocks given. When the learner was in the same room, obedience levels dropped to 40 per cent, and when the participant had to put the learner's hand on the electric plate, obedience dropped to 30 per cent. It seems that taking direct responsibility may reduce obedience.
- The authority figure is removed – when the experimenter left the room, obedience dropped to an average of 20 per cent who shocked to 450 volts. Here again, the participant takes responsibility for his own actions and is less likely to obey instructions.

EVALUATION OF MILGRAM'S RESEARCH

Milgram's studies created enormous interest and concern and have added to our understanding of human behaviour. The ethical issues they raise, such as causing distress and health risks and the use of deception, have contributed to the creation of ethical guidelines to protect participants (see Chapter 15, Ethics).

Although some of the research which replicates Milgram's design does show very similar results, critics argue that the situation was absurd – participants were asked to shock someone, to death if necessary, because they could not remember that 'blue' was paired with 'girl'! Critics such as M. Orne and C. Holland (1968) claim participants did not believe what was happening in the experiment so they relinquished personal responsibility for their actions and relied on the 'experts'. Indeed, if they protested, the experimenter replied 'I'm responsible for what goes on here'. In effect, Milgram was testing participants' trust in, not obedience to, authority.

DEINDIVIDUATION

Have you ever been at a rock concert or football match and felt yourself swept along by the mood of the crowd? If so, you have experienced **deindividuation**, which is the loss of self-awareness and sense of personal responsibility which may occur when we are part of a crowd. As a result of this feeling of anonymity, there are fewer restraints on our behaviour and we are more likely to be impulsive and follow the behaviour of those around us. Deindividuation has been proposed as an explanation for crowd violence.

Figure 3. 6 *Crowd violence*

The notion that being anonymous might allow people to behave more anti-socially was tested by Philip Zimbardo (1969). He had female participants, in groups of four, give 'electric shocks' to his confederates in a learning exercise. In one condition the women wore identical coats and hoods so they were anonymous. In the other condition, the women were individuated – they wore their own clothes, had name tags identifying them and spoke to each other using their own names. Results showed that the anonymous women gave twice as many shocks as the individuated ones and Zimbardo concluded that anonymity permits the release of aggression.

The experiment received criticism because the 'anonymous' women looked like members of the Ku Klux Klan (a group associated with violence towards black people) which may have provided **demand characteristics**. However, in a repeat of the study in which participants wore nurses uniforms, the 'nurses' gave fewer shocks than the individuated participants. This suggests that anonymity is not a major factor in deindividuation, but that uniforms act as a cue, making us more likely to conform to the behaviour they suggest.

FACTORS AFFECTING DEINDIVIDUATION

Research indicates that deindividuation may be affected by:

- **Level of anonymity** – as investigated by Leon Mann's (1981) research. He examined newspaper reports of the behaviour of crowds watching someone threatening to commit suicide by, for instance, jumping from a high building. He found that on some occasions the crowds actually tried to encourage these individuals to jump! This happened when the crowd was large, was in darkness, and was not too close to the person contemplating suicide – all factors which increase anonymity.
- **External cues to behaviour** – such as uniforms or the actions of others. Evidence comes from Zimbardo's study, described on page 33.
- **The mood of the crowd** – people appear to 'pick up' and respond to the mood of the crowd. If, for example, it is happy they will join in the dancing, if it is angry they will throw stones, if it is mournful they will stand quietly.

EVALUATION OF RESEARCH ON DEINDIVIDUATION

One of the problems in researching aggression and other forms of anti-social behaviour is how to measure it in a laboratory setting. The use of the 'electric shock' technique which we have seen above, as well as in Milgram's studies, has been widely used in research. However, the opportunity to give electric shocks is completely unreal, so findings from this research cannot be generalised directly to real life.

Although deindividuation relates to the influence of crowds, it is very difficult to replicate the experience of being in a crowd in the laboratory. As a result, the individual factors thought to affect deindividuation have been studied in isolation. For example, most of the research on anonymity has used groups, not crowds. Crowds are much larger and comprise people from all walks of life who are together for a short time.

SOURCES OF SOCIAL INFLUENCE

Below we review three sources of social influence: group norms, scripts and the media.

GROUP NORMS

A group is a collection of people who have a common identity. This identity may be fairly permanent (an aerobics class or work colleagues) or temporary (people travelling on a bus or a theatre audience). Group norms are the behaviours and attitudes which members of a group expect of each other. These expectations may be unspoken but are nevertheless very powerful, as we saw earlier under Conformity (pp. 27–30).

We conform to group norms for three reasons, according to H. Kelman (1958):

- **compliance** – conforming with the group but not changing our opinion (which occurred in Asch's research)
- **identification** – conforming to group norms but not feeling personally committed to them. Some of the footballers in Figure 3.7 may have felt silly but nevertheless acted in that way as public confirmation of the strength of their group

Figure 3.7 *This team's norm for celebrating success will increase the cohesion of the group*

- **internalisation** – changing our behaviour and opinion to conform to group norms. ✻ This may be because we are not sure what to do, or think (as in Sherif's research), or because we want to be accepted by group members.

SCRIPTS

A **script** is a type of **schema** – a sequence of events and behaviours which occur in a social setting. R. Schank and R. Abelson (1977) proposed that we develop scripts as a way of organising and representing our social knowledge. We are constantly learning new scripts – the five-year-old learns the 'going to school' script, the hospital patient learns the 'being a patient' script and someone made unemployed learns the 'claiming benefit' script.

We learn scripts by watching and listening to others but also by taking part in them. Researchers who studied 'dating' scripts of American students found that those who dated a lot had rich and complex scripts, and could identify behaviour as belonging to a script very easily. Those who dated less had more simple scripts. These results show that although scripts are socially shared experiences, they are also personal, depending on our experience and interests.

Scripts are triggered spontaneously at the start of a script 'sequence', providing us with information about what is expected of us, when we should speak, how we should address someone else, whether we can act casually or formally, and who has power. Scripts therefore influence the way we behave in a social setting. They are also ways of remembering information, so that we assume certain things have happened even though we do not know for sure that they have. This is an example of reconstructive memory, which is discussed further on p. 139.

THE MEDIA

The media provides us with information about our world and, as such, can influence our beliefs and behaviour, for example:

- The 'public interest' and 'public opinion' are presented as though they are something concrete, but there is often little evidence for them. Nevertheless when the media uses these terms it gives the individual the impression that others have this view, and so contributes to the creation of social norms. These may in turn influence people's behaviour and attitudes. It is particularly likely to happen when people are uncertain because, as we have already seen, they look to others for information.

- Stereotypes can be reinforced or weakened by the way people are portrayed in the media. Children are particularly vulnerable to the effects of stereotyping because their knowledge is limited and uncertain. B. Greenberg (1972) found that white children with little everyday contact of black people formed most of their views from the way in which black people were portrayed on television. This indicates the power of the media as an influence on beliefs. The role of the media is explored further under Gender (Chapter 6).

- People working in the media such as newspaper editors and the producers of television programmes are in a position to decide whether or not to publish or broadcast information (such as the private lives of public people or environmental incidents), how important it appears to be (for example front page or bottom of page 11), how it is portrayed (does it show 3,000 peaceful demonstrators or the one scuffle which occurred?), what bias or spin to put on it (are striking health workers 'protesting against the government' or 'concerned about patients' well-being'?). These kinds of decisions affect what information we receive and how we understand it.

Sample Exam Questions

1 Describe one study in which the effects of the presence of other people were investigated, giving the reason why it was conducted, the method used, the results obtained and the conclusion drawn.
(5 marks)

2 Discuss one way in which research into social loafing can be applied to everyday situations.
(3 marks)

3 What is meant by the term deindividuation?
(2 marks)

4 Name one factor which affects conformity.
(1 mark)

5 Describe one study in which obedience was investigated, giving the reason why it was conducted, the method used, the results obtained and the conclusion drawn.
(5 marks)

6 Using your knowledge of psychology, describe one source of social influence.
(3 marks)

Attachment and Separation

The newborn infant is utterly dependent on others if it is to survive – others provide food, warmth and protection. This helplessness seems to act like a magnet, attracting the adult's attention and care. The material in this chapter shows how psychologists have studied the development of the relationship between a baby and its carers and its importance for the child's long term well-being. We also look at what happens to the child if this bond is damaged or broken.

ATTACHMENTS

An attachment can be defined as a strong emotional bond between two people. Infant behaviours such as crying, making eye contact, reaching and grasping form the basis of its interaction with others. These behaviours invite carers to respond to the baby; to interact with it and thus form an attachment. As we will see shortly, attachments seem to be important for many aspects of a baby's long term development.

THE DEVELOPMENT OF ATTACHMENTS

A baby's attachments develop in the following sequence:

- **Up to 3 months of age** – indiscriminate attachments. Most babies respond equally to any caregiver.
- **After 4 months** – preference for certain people, usually those it is more familiar with, so a baby may wave its arms or smile when it sees its father's face, but there will be little reaction from the baby when it sees a stranger.
- **After 7 months** – special preference. The baby looks to particular people for security, comfort and protection. It shows fear of strangers (**stranger fear**) and unhappiness when separated from a special person (**separation anxiety**). Some babies show stranger fear and separation anxiety much more frequently and intensely than others, but nevertheless they are seen as evidence that the baby has formed an attachment. This has usually developed by one year of age.
- **After 9 months** – multiple attachments. The baby becomes increasingly independent and forms several attachments.

Figure 4.1 *This baby is showing stranger fear*

Research on the development of attachments was conducted by Rudi Schaffer and Peggy Emerson (1964). The babies were visited monthly for approximately one year, their interactions with their carers were observed, and carers were interviewed. Evidence for the development of an attachment was that the baby showed separation anxiety after a carer left.

The results indicated that attachments were most likely to form with those who responded accurately to the baby's signals, not the person they spent most time with. Schaffer and Emerson called this **sensitive responsiveness**. Many of the babies had several attachments by 10 months old, including attachments to mothers, fathers, grandparents, siblings and neighbours. The mother was the main attachment figure for about half of the children at 18 months old and the father for most of the others.

SECURE AND INSECURE ATTACHMENTS

By the 'security' of the child's attachment we mean how confident the child is that its special person will provide what it needs. The security of attachment in one- to two-year-olds was investigated by Mary Ainsworth and her colleagues (1978) in the 'strange situation' research.

She observed children's behaviour when mothers and strangers came into and left the room the child was in and when the child was left alone. She concluded that the type of attachment children showed could be classed as either secure or insecure, but there were two types of insecurity. The three types of attachment behaviours noted by Ainsworth were:

- **Securely attached** – happy when mother present; distressed by her absence; went to her quickly when she returned; a stranger provided little comfort.
- **Insecurely attached – anxious avoidant** – avoided the mother; indifferent to her presence or absence; the child showed greatest distress when alone; a stranger could comfort just as well as the mother.
- **Insecurely attached – anxious resistant** – seemed unsure of mother; more anxious about mother's presence; distressed in her absence; would go to her quickly when she returned then struggle to get away; also resisted strangers.

The percentage of children in her sample which showed each of the three attachment types are shown in Table 4.1.

Type of attachment	Approximate percentage of children
Securely attached	65%
Insecurely attached – anxious avoidant	23%
Insecurely attached – anxious resistant	12%

Table 4.1 *Ainsworth's three types of attachment*

A third type of insecure attachment was identified by M. Main and J. Soloman (1985) which they called **disorganised attachment**. Children appeared to be dazed or confused, and they showed avoidance and clinging at the same time.

Securely attached babies tend to have experienced sensitive and responsive caring. Parents accept the baby and provide care which is consistent. Radke-Yarrow and colleagues (1985) found that babies rated as insecure–avoidant were more likely to have mothers who were psychologically unavailable to their infants, showing signs of depression and some reluctance for physical contact with their babies.

However, Ainsworth's conclusion that the **strange situation** can be used to identify the child's type of attachment has been criticised on the grounds that it identifies only the type of attachment to the mother. The child may have a different type of attachment to the father or grandmother, for example. In addition, some research has shown that the same child may show different attachment behaviours on different occasions. Children's attachments may change, perhaps because of changes in the child's circumstances, so a securely attached child may appear insecurely attached if the mother becomes ill or the family circumstances change.

EFFECTS OF SECURE AND INSECURE ATTACHMENTS

Ainsworth suggested that insecure attachments may contribute to the development of poor adult relationships and poor intellectual development. Equally, a secure attachment appears to contribute to better social and emotional development. M. Erickson and colleagues (1985) observed four- to five-year-olds in pre-school settings. They rated the children on how confidently and assertively they approached tasks and activities, level of dependence on the teacher and social skills with other children. These children had already been rated for the security or insecurity of their attachments at one year old, so Erickson was able to compare the ratings of securely attached children with those who were insecurely attached. The results are shown in Table 4.2.

Type of attachment	Confidence in tasks	Dependency on teacher	Social skills
Securely attached	4.5	2.7	4.1
Insecurely attached	3.6	3.5	3.2

Table 4.2 *Average ratings of various behaviours of securely and insecurely attached children (Erickson et al., 1985)*

The conclusions from this study are that securely attached children become more confident and socially skilled and less dependent by four or five years old. Helen Bee (1989) proposed that the distinction between the two types of attachment plays an important role in predicting a wide range of other differences between children. She summarises findings from research on children up to about six years old. In addition to the differences shown in Table 4.2, these findings show differences in:

- **self-esteem** – securely attached children have higher self-esteem at four to five years old
- **tantrums and aggressive behaviour** – insecurely attached children show more of this behaviour
- **empathy** – securely attached children show more empathy towards other children and adults. They do not show pleasure on seeing others' distress, which is fairly common among children with an anxious–avoidant attachment
- **problem solving** – securely attached toddlers show longer attention span and use the mother more effectively when they need help
- **play** – at 18-30 months of age, securely attached children show more mature and complex play.

PRACTICAL APPLICATIONS OF THE WORK ON ATTACHMENTS

The work on attachment has highlighted its importance in children's development. From this work we can summarise some of the lessons to be learned about how attachments can be encouraged and protected in the care of young children. New parents are developing their parenting skills, just as their babies are developing their attachments. Below are some of the ways in which parents can encourage and support their baby's attachments.

- Be available and responsive to the baby.
- Be sensitive to the baby's needs, so that your responses are appropriate to its age, mood and needs.
- Be warm and accepting.
- Be consistent in your responses because this provides security and predictability.
- Encourage the development of attachments to other people, using these pointers.
- If the baby has to be separated from an attached figure, ensure as much warmth and consistency in care as possible and maintain high quality contact with other attached figures.

DEPRIVATION, PRIVATION AND SEPARATION

These terms refer to the circumstances which can damage attachments. We will start by looking at the ideas of John Bowlby, who was working from the 1940s until the 1980s.

BOWLBY'S MATERNAL DEPRIVATION HYPOTHESIS

Bowlby was a psychoanalyst, believing that early experiences have a profound effect on later life. Outlined below is some of the research which formed the basis for his views.

BOWLBY'S RESEARCH

Bowlby (1946) was working with emotionally disturbed juveniles (young people) during the 1940s and as part of this work he investigated their early years using the **case study** method. This involved interviews and looking at past school and medical records. Bowlby divided the young people into two groups with 44 participants in each. One group comprised juvenile thieves, the other consisted of juveniles who were emotionally disturbed but had no known criminal involvement.

His results showed that more than half of the juvenile thieves had been separated from their mothers for longer than six months during their first five years. In the other group only two had had such a separation. He also found several of the young thieves showed 'affectionless psychopathy' (they were not able to care about or feel affection for others). Bowlby concluded that the reason for the anti-social behaviour and emotional problems in the first group was due to **maternal deprivation.**

THE CASE STUDY

The use of the case study in research brings some weaknesses. It relies on people's memory of the past which is often biased and partial, as we know from memory research (see Chapter 12). People reconstruct their memories, they may be unable to retrieve memories for traumatic events, and the way they are questioned may lead them to give biased answers. In addition, the written records of someone's medical or school history may be incomplete or written for a purpose that differs from the researcher's aim.

Understanding Psychology

Critics say that Bowlby's results may have been biased because of weaknesses in the case study method (see above). There was also a basic error in the design of Bowlby's research which makes his conclusions invalid. It appeared that a large proportion of maternally deprived children became juvenile thieves simply because one of his groups consisted of participants who were already juvenile thieves. To test the effect of maternal deprivation he should have compared a group who had experienced separation from their mothers with a matched group who had had no separation. If there was a difference in the outcomes between the two groups, he could then have concluded that it was due to maternal deprivation.

THE ROBERTSON'S RESEARCH

Immediately after separation, children may experience the **distress syndrome**. This is a particular pattern of behaviours revealed, for example, by James and Joyce Robertson (1969). They observed and filmed 17-month-old John when he was separated from his mother whilst she was in hospital. During his 9 days in a residential nursery they noted these three stages of distress:

- **protest** – the child cries, protests and shows physical agitation
- **despair** – the child is miserable and listless; he shows signs of depression
- **detachment** – the child seems to accept the situation and shows little interest when reunited with the attached figure. He may actively resist contact with the attached figure, struggling to be put down if cuddled, for example.

Figure 4.2 *Which stage of distress is John showing in this photo?*

This distress sydrome has been noted by other researchers, but the one observed by the Robertsons followed the child's separation from his mother when he was not provided with a fully available substitute mother.

GOLDFARB'S RESEARCH

Goldfarb (1943) studied the development of children who spent their early months in an orphanage. He compared one group who were fostered in the first year with another group who remained there for another two years. Results showed that at 12 years of age, both groups showed emotional problems. However, when compared with those who left early, those who stayed longer in the orphanage scored lower on IQ tests and sociability, and showed higher levels of aggressive behaviour. Goldfarb concluded that this poorer development was due to their time in the institution, where no attachment figures were available to them.

THE NATURAL EXPERIMENT
Goldfarb's research can be classed as a natural experiment. Can you explain why?

This research has been criticised because it did not fully consider the reasons why some children were fostered at an early age and others were not. It could have been that the more responsive children were fostered, which is why they showed higher levels of sociability and intelligence at 12 years of age.

Bowlby argued that these studies provided evidence that maternal attachment was as important for a child's psychological health as vitamins and proteins were for its physical health. He proposed that the attachment to the mother forms the basis for all future relationships and is unique in its quality and its importance. His **maternal deprivation hypothesis** says that if a child does not develop a strong, unbroken attachment with its mother (or permanent mother substitute) during its first three years, or if the attachment is broken, then the child will develop long term social, emotional and intellectual problems.

Bowlby's theory offered a comprehensive explanation for the development of attachments and stressed the importance of attachments for a child's long term development. His evidence was crucial in changing childcare practices in, for example, hospitals. Emphasis shifted towards the emotional needs of the child; parents were encouraged to be with the child in hospital, and nursing care and the ward itself became child-centred.

MATERNAL DEPRIVATION UNPACKED

In a reassessment of Bowlby's ideas, Michael Rutter (1982) put forward the view that Bowlby's emphasis on the importance of attachment behaviour and bonding was correct, but that he was wrong to identify the mother as the crucial factor. In particular, Rutter asserts that the damaging influences Bowlby cited were due to a variety of circumstances, not simply to **maternal deprivation**. In addition, Bowlby used the term 'maternal deprivation' to refer to separation from an attached figure, loss of an attached figure and failure to develop an attachment to any figure. These each have different effects, argued Rutter.

SEPARATION
After filming John's **separation** from his mother (see p. 42), the Robertsons concluded that his distress could have been due to one or more of the following variables:

- being in a strange and stressful environment
- being deprived of maternal care (that is, warm and affectionate attention)
- being separated from his mother.

Understanding Psychology

The Robertsons subsequently cared for two girls during a temporary separation from their mothers. Each girl visited them with her mother before the mother went into hospital. The Robertsons made sure that the care they gave was similar to the mother's – similar routine and plenty of individual attention. One of the Robertsons was always present to look after and comfort the child, and each child brought mementos from home and was encouraged to talk about her mother. In these ways the first two of the variables listed above were eliminated, so the Robertsons were able to study the effect of the last variable – physical separation from the mother.

Results showed that each girl experienced mild distress but otherwise adapted well to the change. The Robertsons concluded that this was because the new situation was familiar and that both children formed an attachment to their new carers. In addition, keeping the child's memory of the mother alive prevented disruption to the bond. However, these conclusions can be criticised because the children were girls and the original study was of a boy; gender differences could have accounted for the lower level of distress shown. In addition, these are all **case studies** so we cannot **generalise** the results to the population as a whole.

This study underlines one of Rutter's points, that the short term effects of separation may be due to an unfamiliar environment. In addition, as we saw from research by Schaffer and Emerson on p. 38, children can form several attachments which may protect them against distress when separated from one attached figure.

Figure 4.3 *Children who have several attachments will be better able to withstand the effects of bond disruption with one of their attached figures*

In the long term, the effects of separation may include:

- the child's attachment becoming more insecure, so the child clings to the attached figure;
- the child showing separation anxiety for a year or longer or becoming detached.

DEPRIVATION

Bowlby used the term maternal deprivation to refer to the separation or loss of the mother as well as failure to develop an attachment. Michael Rutter (1981) argued that if a child fails to develop an attachment this is **privation**, whereas deprivation refers to the loss of or damage to an attachment. We will therefore consider these two separately.

In Rutter's view, **deprivation** occurs when the child's attachment is damaged or broken due to either separation from the attached figure, or loss of the attached figure, for instance through divorce or death. There may be short and long term effects of deprivation. We have considered the short term effects earlier, but Rutter views the reasons for the loss of an attachment as crucial in the explanation of long term effects.

Rutter's (1976) evidence from his own research on the long term effects of early separation from mothers reveals the importance of the home environment and previous experiences. His sample comprised 9–12-year-old boys from London and from the Isle of Wight. He looked particularly at anti-social behaviour. His results indicated that:

- there was more anti-social behaviour in boys from families where the parents' marriage was rated as 'very poor' or where parent–child relationships were cold or neglectful
- there was no difference in anti-social behaviour between boys who had separated from one parent and those who had separated from both parents
- when a parent died, a child was only slightly more likely to become delinquent than a child from an 'intact' home
- boys who were separated because of illness or housing problems did not become maladjusted.

Rutter concluded that there was no correlation between separation experiences and delinquency. He argued that delinquency is not caused by disruption of the bond (as Bowlby claimed) because when disruption was final with the death of a parent, there was only a slight increase in delinquency.

Rutter did find that there was a correlation between family discord and delinquency, suggesting that family discord (such as arguing, lack of affection, stress) created a distortion of family relationships. Rutter argued that this was not particularly related to early childhood, as Bowlby claimed. The distorted relationships may be linked to **insecure attachments**, perhaps even preventing the formation of attachments (privation).

Rutter noted that the long term effects of deprivation showed:

- an increase in anti-social behaviour where the separation had been related to family discord or a history of disturbance in the life of the young person
- children with secure attachments and those who had experienced successful separations previously seemed to be able to withstand the effects of deprivation more than a child whose attachments were insecure

- children differ in their ability to cope with the effects of deprivation; boys appear to be more vulnerable to these effects than girls, as do children between seven months and three years of age.

PRIVATION

Privation occurs when there is a failure to form an attachment to any individual, perhaps because the child has a series of different carers (which was the case for many of Bowlby's juvenile thieves) or family discord prevents the development of attachment to any figure (as Rutter proposed). Privated children do not show distress when separated from a familiar figure, which indicates a lack of attachment.

From his survey of research on privation, Rutter proposed that it is likely to lead initially to clinging, dependent behaviour, attention-seeking and indiscriminate friendliness, then as the child matures, an inability to keep rules, form lasting relationships, or feel guilt. He also found evidence of anti-social behaviour, affectionless psychopathy, and disorders of language, intellectual development and physical growth.

Rutter argues that these problems are not due solely to the lack of attachment to a mother figure, as Bowlby claimed, but to factors such as the lack of intellectual stimulation and social experiences which attachments normally provide. In addition, such problems can be overcome later in the child's development, with the right kind of care.

Evidence for this comes from research by Jill Hodges and Barbara Tizard (1989). They followed the development of children who had been in residential nurseries from only a few months old. The care provided was of good quality, but carers were discouraged from forming attachments with the children. At about three years of age some children were adopted, some returned to their mothers, the rest remained in the nursery. They were also compared with a control group, who had spent all their lives in their own families. The children were assessed at two, four, and eight years old.

At two years of age none of the institutionalised children had formed attachments, but by eight years of age those who were adopted had formed good attachments. Also their social and intellectual development was better than that of children returned to their own families. Those returned to their families showed more behavioural problems and the attachments were weaker. Nevertheless all those children who had spent their early years in institutions were more attention-seeking from adults and showed some difficulties in their social relationships, particularly with their peers.

Some of these children were interviewed again at 16 years of age, as were their parents and care-workers. They were compared with a new control group as the original control children no longer matched the children in the adopted and restored groups.

SAMPLING AND A MATCHED PAIRS DESIGN
In order to obtain the control group, Hodges and Tizard approached 53 GP practices, 16 of which agreed to write to the families of 16-year-olds asking them to help in a study of adolescents and their families. Approximately 30 per cent of the families receiving this request said they did not wish to be contacted. The participants for the comparison

group were selected from the remainder, to be matched with the experimental groups.

The comparison group comprised 16-year-olds, each one matched with the adopted and the restored participants on the basis of sex, one- or two-parent family, occupational classification of the main breadwinner and position in the family. Those with a mental or physical disability or who had spent extended periods away from the family were excluded.

Hodges and Tizard found that the adopted children still had good attachments which compared favourably with the control children. Fewer restored children were reported as having good attachments but the children who had been brought up in institutional care had experienced most instability and showed some difficulties in their later attachments.

We can conclude from this evidence that Bowlby was correct to emphasise the importance of the early years, but the effects of delay in the formation of attachments do not necessarily persist into adulthood and lead to affectionless psychopathy, as Bowlby predicted.

However, Hodges and Tizard used **interviews** and **questionnaires**, both of which can produce answers that are affected by **social desirability** – the wish to appear in a good light. The responses of those interviewed may have been inaccurate, and this would affect the results.

Another difficulty in this research is that six of the original 51 families of eight-year-olds refused to take part in this later research. It could be that families experiencing more difficulties were more likely to refuse, and this may also apply to the comparison group, because the families who agreed to take part may have been those with fairly good relationships with their 16-year-olds. Thus, the results of the research may be biased due to the sample.

Sample Exam Questions

1 **Describe one study in which attachment in children has been investigated.**
   (5 marks)

2 **Using your knowledge of psychology, discuss two ways of encouraging the development of a child's attachment.**
   (6 marks)

3 **Identify two of the beneficial effects of a secure attachment.**
   (2 marks)

4 **Describe one possible short term effect of separation from an attached figure.**
   (3 marks)

5 **What do psychologists mean by privation?**
   (2 marks)

6 **Outline one possible long term effect on children of breaking attachment bonds.**
   (3 marks)

CHAPTER 5

Cognitive Development

Imagine that someone showed you two pieces of string side by side, of the same length, and then scrunched one up. You would know it was still the same length as the other one, but a four-year-old child would not. This shows that our understanding of the world changes as we grow up; we think about things in a different way. This change in our thinking is called cognitive development.

PIAGET'S THEORY OF INTELLECTUAL DEVELOPMENT

In Jean Piaget's early work with children he asked them questions, and was interested to find that when children gave the wrong answers they were often the same kind of wrong answers. As a result of further research Piaget proposed that children's thinking is different from adults, and their thinking develops in stages from infancy to adulthood. He argued that this development is biologically based, and changes as the child matures. Therefore, according to his view, **cognition** develops in all children in these same stages. Before we examine these stages, we will look at some important features of Piaget's theory:

- **Schema** – this is a mental framework; an internal representation of an action, object, person, situation, idea or concept. Piaget called the schema the basic building block of intelligent behaviour – a way of organising knowledge. For example, a baby has a schema for grasping – it wraps its fingers around anything which is put in the palm of its hand. Schemas enable us to organise, store and interpret information about our experiences.
- **Adaptation** – cognitive development is a process of adaptation to our environment. As an infant matures and interacts with its environment, the schemas become more complex and new ones develop. Adaptation can be defined as using existing knowledge to make sense of situations, and changing this knowledge when existing knowledge is inadequate. Adaptation occurs through two processes which Piaget called assimilation and accommodation.
- **Assimilation** – initially, a baby will use its grasping schema for getting hold of fingers, but it will then begin to grasp rattles or blankets. The child uses its schema to interact with these new objects. Assimilation can therefore be defined as the process of incorporating our experiences into already existing schemas.

- **Accommodation** – there are times when a baby's schema is inadequate for what it is trying to do. The baby in Figure 5.1 would be unable to hold the ball by using the grasping schema: her existing knowledge has had to change. Now she can hold her hands flat (although you can see the remains of grasping in her third finger) and co-ordinate both hands in order to hold the ball. This is an example of accommodation, which can be defined as the process of modifying existing schema in order to meet the demands of new experiences.

Figure 5.1 *This baby now has a schema for holding*

- **Equilibration** – when a child has assimilated the schemas for all its experiences, it is in a state of equilibrium, or cognitive balance. But because of its continuing exploration of its world it will come across new experiences which will create cognitive imbalance. Equilibration is the process of restoring balance: the need to regain equilibrium is what drives the child to change its thinking in order to make sense of new information. Piaget viewed intelligence as the extent to which a person can adapt to a changing environment and maintain equilibrium.

PIAGET'S FOUR STAGES OF INTELLECTUAL DEVELOPMENT

Piaget proposed that a child's understanding develops through four stages – these are described below along with their characteristics.

SENSORIMOTOR STAGE

From birth, a baby explores its world using its senses (sight, sound, taste, touch and so on) in combination with body movements. Initially these movements are simple, for example the baby watches a moving object, reaches out towards it and after many attempts is able to grasp the object. After a number of tries the baby will then bring the object to its mouth, and explore it using its sense of taste and smell, as we saw in Figure 5.1.

OBJECT PERMANENCE

One of the chief characteristics of the sensorimotor stage is **object permanence**. This is Piaget's term for a child's understanding that an object still exists even when it is not visible. He found that when five- or six-month-old babies were playing with a toy, they immediately lost interest if the toy was covered with a cloth. It seemed, to the baby, as though the object never existed (see Figure 5.2).

Figure 5.2 *This child loses interest in the toy directly it is covered up*

When Piaget did the same thing with a ten-month-old, the baby continued to reach for the toy, sometimes showing distress that it had disappeared. From this behaviour Piaget inferred that the child had achieved object permanence; it had a mental representation (a schema) of the object.

CRITICAL RESEARCH

Tom Bower and Jennifer Wishart (1972) argued that objects do still exist in a baby's mind, even though they are not visible. Their research used babies less than four months old who were filmed in a laboratory using an infra-red camera. A toy was offered to the baby, but as it reached for the toy, the light in the laboratory was switched off. The infra-red camera showed that the baby continued to reach for the toy, even though it was no longer visible.

One explanation for Piaget's findings is that the baby is distracted by the movement of the cover as it is placed over the rattle, which is why it looks away and appears to 'forget' having been interested in the rattle. By eliminating the distracting movement, Bower and Wishart's research revealed that the baby continued to reach, suggesting that children as young as four months of age have object permanence.

PRE-OPERATIONAL STAGE

During its second year, a toddler starts to use symbols or signs to represent things. This is called **symbolic thinking** and it is evident when a child makes a cardboard box 'stand for' a house or a car. Language is evidence of symbolic thinking, because a child knows that when you say 'table' the word 'stands for' an actual table – he could draw one, or point one out in the room, or tell you how you could use a table. Piaget said that language skills develop as a result of a child's cognitive development.

EGOCENTRISM

Another characteristic of this stage is egocentrism. Have you ever played 'hide and seek' with a three-year-old who hides by standing in front of you and covering his eyes? Because he cannot see you he thinks you cannot see him. Piaget argued that from birth a child has understood the world only from his own viewpoint so he thinks others have the same views and experiences as he does. Piaget called this egocentrism: the child is unable to understand the world from the point of view of another person.

Piaget and his colleagues devised the 'three mountains task' to test children's ego-centric thinking (see Figure 5.3). A child sat at a large, table-top model of three mountains and was asked what he could see from his side of the table. A doll was then placed at various positions around the table. The child was shown photographs of the mountains taken from these different positions, and asked to indicate which of them showed the doll's view.

Most four- and five-year-old children pointed to photographs which showed their own view. This suggests they thought the doll's view would be the same as their own, which indicates egocentrism. However, most seven-year-olds identified the doll's view correctly. We can conclude that by this age a child understands it is possible for there to be two different views of the same thing at the same time; their thinking is no longer egocentric.

Figure 5.3 *A child doing the 'three mountains task'*

Egocentric thinking is an example of **centration**. Piaget used this term for a child's tendency to focus on only one feature of a situation. The child seems to be unable to represent both features of a situation to himself at any one time. We will look further at centration in the next stage of cognitive development.

CRITICAL RESEARCH

Martin Hughes (1975) argued that the three mountains task did not make sense to the children and was made more difficult because the children had to match the doll's view with a photograph. Hughes devised a task which made sense to the child. He showed children a model comprising two intersecting walls, a 'boy' doll and a 'policeman' doll. He then placed the policeman doll in various positions and asked the child to hide the boy doll from the policeman. Hughes did this to make sure that the child understood what was being asked of him, so if he made mistakes they were explained and the child tried again. Interestingly, very few mistakes were made.

The experiment then began. Hughes brought in a second policeman doll, and placed both dolls at the end of two walls, as shown in Figure 5.4.

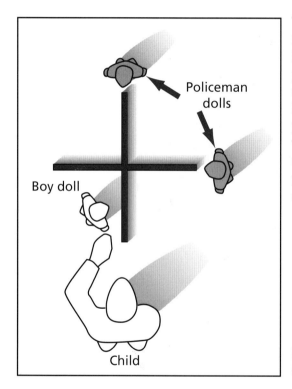

The child was asked to hide the boy from both policemen, in other words he had to take account of two different points of view. Hughes' sample comprised children between three and a half and five years of age, of whom 90 per cent gave correct answers. Even when he devised a more complex situation, with more walls and a third policeman, 90 per cent of four-year-olds were successful.

Figure 5.4 *The layout of Hughes' experiment on egocentrism*

This shows that children have largely lost their egocentric thinking by four years of age, because they are able to take the view of another. Hughes' experiment allowed them to demonstrate this because the task made sense to the child, whereas Piaget's did not.

CONCRETE OPERATIONAL STAGE

A child has entered this stage when they are able to **conserve**. This means that the child understands that although the appearance of something changes, the thing itself does not. The scrunched up piece of string, described at the start of this chapter, is an example of the conservation of length.

CONSERVATION

By seven years of age the majority of children can conserve liquid, because they understand that when water is poured into a different shaped glass, the quantity of liquid remains the same even though its appearance has changed. As illustrated in Figure 5.5, the child is first asked 'Is there the same amount of liquid in this one and this one?'. After the liquid has been poured into the different shaped glass the question is repeated.

Five-year-olds would think there was a different amount because the appearance had changed, but seven-year-olds would answer correctly, justifying their answer by saying that if the liquid was poured back into the original glass it would be at the same level. This is called **reversibility**, and is evidence that the child can use abstract reasoning; can represent information to himself and therefore manipulate it.

Conservation of liquid

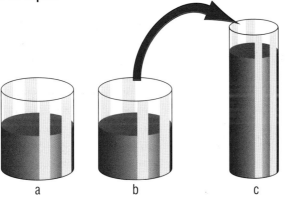

                    a   b   c

1. Two identical glasses of liquid (a and b).
2. b is poured into c.

Conservation of number

Child's row

Adult's row

Adult's row
arranged

Figure 5.5 *Piaget's tasks to test conservation of liquid and number*

Conservation of number develops soon after this, as demonstrated in research by Piaget and his colleagues and illustrated in Figure 5.5. Piaget set out a row of counters in front of the child and asked her to make another row the same as the first one. Piaget then spread out his row of counters and asked the child if there were still the same number. Most seven-year-olds answered correctly, and Piaget concluded that this showed that by seven years of age children were able to conserve number.

However, a younger child was more likely to say there were more counters in the longer row. The child is still showing centration, focusing on the fact that the rows look different. When he is able, at the same time, to notice that no counters have been added or taken away, then he comes to the correct conclusion. He can take into account more than one feature of a situation; he can **decentre**.

CRITICAL RESEARCH

Several aspects of the conservation tasks have been criticised, for example that they fail to take account of the social context of the child's understanding. Susan Rose and Marion Blank (1974) argued that when a child gives the wrong answer to a question, we repeat the question in order to hint that their first answer was wrong. This is what Piaget did by asking children the same question twice in the conservation experiments, before and after the transformation. When Rose and Blank replicated this but asked the question only once, after the liquid had been poured, they found many more six-year-olds gave the correct answer. This shows children can conserve at a younger age than Piaget claimed.

Another feature of the conservation task which may interfere with children's understanding is that the adult purposely alters the appearance of something, so the child thinks this alteration is important. James McGarrigle and Margaret Donaldson (1974) devised a study of conservation of number in which the alteration was accidental.

When two identical rows of sweets were laid out and the child was satisfied there were the same number in each, a 'naughty teddy' appeared. Whilst playing around, teddy actually messed up one row of sweets. Once he was safely back in a box the children were asked if there were the same number of sweets. The children were between four- and six-years-old, and more than half gave the correct answer. This suggests that, once again, Piaget's design prevented the children from showing that they can conserve at a younger age than he claimed.

CLASSIFICATION

Piaget also studied children's ability to classify objects – to put them together on the basis of their colour or shape, for example. He found that children in the pre-operational stage had difficulty in understanding that a class can include a number of sub-classes. For example, a child is shown four red flowers and two white ones and is then asked 'Are there more red flowers or more flowers?'. A typical five-year-old would say 'more red ones'.

Despite this, Piaget found that the child understood that if you took away all the red flowers then the white ones would be left, and also that if you took away all the flowers none would be left. This shows that the child knows what the words mean, but seems unable to distinguish between the class (all the flowers) and the sub-class (flowers of the same colour).

This is called **class inclusion**, and Piaget explained these results by saying that the child centres on one aspect, either class or sub-class. It is not until he can **decentre** that he can simultaneously compare both the whole and the parts which make up the whole. He can then understand the relationship between class and sub-class.

CRITICAL RESEARCH

James McGarrigle designed a study which tested Piaget's explanation that a child is unable to compare class with sub-class because of centration. He used four toy cows, three were black and one was white. He laid all the cows on their side and told the child they were 'sleeping'. McGarrigle argued that by using 'sleeping' he increased the emphasis on all the cows – the whole class. He asked children two questions, which are shown in Table 5.1. The first question was comparable to Piaget's.

Question	Percentage of children answering correctly
'Are there more black cows or more cows?'	25%
'Are there more black cows or more sleeping cows?'	48%

Table 5.1 *The results of McGarrigle's study on class inclusion*

The average age of the children was six years, and McGarrigle concluded that it was the way Piaget worded his question that prevented the younger children from showing that they understood the relationship between class and sub-class.

FORMAL OPERATIONAL STAGE

Most of the characteristics described in the previous stage have developed by about 11 years of age. The child shows logical thinking but generally needs to be able to work through sequences with actual objects (which is why it is called the **concrete operational** stage). Once the child can manipulate ideas in its head, without any dependence on concrete manipulation, it has entered the **formal operational** stage. It can do mathematical calculations, think creatively and imagine the outcome of particular actions.

An example of the distinction between the concrete and formal operational stages is the answer to the question 'If Kelly is taller than Ali and Ali is taller than Jo, who is tallest?'. This is an example of **inferential reasoning**, which is the ability to think about things which the child has not actually experienced and to draw conclusions from this thinking. Children who can reason the answer out in their heads are using formal operational thinking. The child who needs to draw a picture or use objects is still in the concrete operational stage.

Piaget tested formal operational thinking by giving children the pendulum task, which is illustrated in Figure 5.6.

The child is given string and a set of weights, and told she can:
- *change the weights;*
- *change the length of the string;*
- *vary the strength of her 'push'.*

Her task is to find out which of these factors affects the time taken to complete one swing of the 'pendulum'.

Children in the formal operational stage approached the task systematically, testing one variable (such as varying the length of the string) at a time to see its effect. However, younger children typically tried out these variations randomly or changed two things at the same time. Piaget concluded that the systematic approach indicated the children were thinking logically, in the abstract, and could see the relationships between things. These are the characteristics of the formal operational stage.

Figure 5.6 *Piaget's pendulum task for formal operational thinking*

CRITICAL RESEARCH

Psychologists who have replicated this research, or used a similar problem, have generally found that children cannot complete the task successfully until they are older. Robert Siegler (1979) gave children a balance beam task in which some discs were placed either side of the centre of balance. The researcher changed the number of discs or moved them along the beam, each time asking the child to predict which way the balance would go.

He studied the answers given by children from five years upwards, concluding that they apply rules which develop in the same sequence as, and thus reflect, Piaget's findings. Like Piaget, he found that eventually the children were able to take into account the interaction between the weight of the discs and the distance from the centre, and so successfully predict balance. However, this did not happen until participants were between 13 and 17 years of age. He concluded that children's cognitive development is based on acquiring and using rules in increasingly more complex situations, rather than in stages.

A CRITICAL APPRAISAL OF PIAGET'S THEORY

Piaget's theory has generated considerable research and criticism. We will review the criticism before assessing his contribution to the study of cognitive development.

METHODOLOGY

Piaget has been criticised for various aspects of his methods, one of which was the naturalistic observation.

NATURALISTIC OBSERVATION
Piaget used naturalistic observations of his own children when they were only a few weeks old, which is an example of research in a natural setting. The tendency for observers to be biased can be counteracted by using two or more observers, but Piaget observed and made notes alone. Generalisations should not be made from research such as this, but Piaget did generalise and many of his ideas on sensorimotor and pre-operational stages are based on these observations.

Piaget also used **clinical interviews** to study the thinking of children, but his questions and methods were not standardised. Although children were asked the same question initially, subsequent questions related to the individual child's answers. This may 'lead' the children to give the kinds of answers the researcher is looking for. Piaget did use experiments in his later work, with standardised tasks and instructions, but the sample size was small.

We have seen in some of the critical research that his underestimation of a child's social understanding biased the results he found. The child's perception of adults, the meaning of a second question and the importance of a familiar context all affect children's performance. Margaret Donaldson (1978) is one of several researchers who have noted the willingness of their young participants to oblige the adult researcher. The child sees the experiment as a social situation involving a child and an adult; the researcher sees it as an experiment involving a participant and a researcher.

PIAGET'S CONCLUSIONS

Criticism of Piaget's conclusions have included the following:

- Changes in children's thinking occur at an earlier age than Piaget claimed. It seems that weaknesses in his research prevented children from showing what they did in fact understand.
- Piaget may have overestimated the age at which children enter the formal operational stage.
- Because Piaget concentrated on the individual child, he failed to consider the effect that the social setting may have on cognitive development. The way that adults use language and gestures and the child's experience through social interactions are very influential.
- Development is continuous rather than stage-like because the move from one stage to the next is not clear cut. Therefore understanding may be apparent in one task but not in another, as occurs with conservation. A child can understand a task which is clear and relevant to its experience (as in Hughes' experiment) but be

unable to complete a more complex version of the same task (the three mountains task) until it is quite a bit older.

SUMMARY

Despite these criticisms, the abilities which Piaget identified, and the sequence in which they develop, have been largely substantiated, although he did underestimate the ages at which children achieved particular types of understanding. This is due in part to the issue of competence versus performance, which refers to the difficulty of finding out what children actually understand – a difficulty which is common to any research with children and which the critical research we have examined has tried to overcome.

Piaget's theory is not so much an explanation for cognitive development as a description of it. However, it has generated a huge amount of research which has furthered our understanding. Piaget did modify some aspects of his theory over several decades as a result of further research. He used these principles to explain other aspects of development, including moral development (see p. 74).

His theory has been very influential, and his view of children as active learners and his practical ideas have been used widely to enrich children's cognitive development, a point we turn to now.

APPLICATIONS OF PIAGETIAN PRINCIPLES

Those who work with children can use Piaget's principles in a variety of ways. Some examples are explored below.

DISCOVERY LEARNING

Children learn best by discovering things for themselves. Piaget felt that the purpose of education was to help children become autonomous learners, to construct their own understanding and become able to solve problems for themselves. The role of those working with children is to support discovery learning. They need to set tasks which interest the child, and which challenge her, so that disequilibrium is created. The child must then accommodate this new information but also needs opportunity for assimilation. This requires toys, activities and materials which will allow the child to apply the new schema to its environment.

As an example, a three-year-old who is playing with a plastic container in a bowl of water could be given two or three more containers of different sizes. The adult could suggest pouring water from one to the other, offering the child different sized containers. The adult could comment on what happens when water from a large container overflows a smaller one. Why is the water falling out of the small container, but not the large container? This is an example of disequilibrium and this challenges the child to think about what she is experiencing.

READINESS

Those working with children need to know each child's level of cognitive development so that appropriate toys or materials are available for the child to explore. For children at the sensorimotor stage, an example would be stacking toys. In school, teachers can set tasks which are appropriate to each child's abilities. For example, because a child develops conservation of number before conservation of volume, principles relating to number should be introduced before those relating to volume.

Piaget asserts that children come to understand new concepts through concrete experiences. Teachers should ensure that there are plenty of resources available for children to classify, to count, to share out and so on, which will help them understand adding and dividing. Resources may include small coloured blocks for counting or different lengths and colours of rod for measuring.

DECENTRING

Decentring can be encouraged by giving a child the opportunity to hear or see things from other people's perspectives. When a group of children work together they have to listen to other ideas and try to solve problems which satisfy everyone. Adults can also play an important role by pointing out another feature of a situation and encouraging the child to consider it.

Sample Exam Questions

1 Describe the role of accommodation in the development of schema.
   (3 marks)

2 Identify one characteristic of the sensorimotor stage of development.
   (2 marks)

3 What is meant by the term 'conservation'?
   (2 marks)

4 a What conclusion can be drawn from Table 5.1 showing the results of McGarrigle's study? *(1 mark)*
  b Explain your answer. *(2 marks)*

5 Describe one study in which inferential reasoning was investigated, including the method used, the results obtained and the conclusions drawn.
   (4 marks)

6 Use your knowledge of psychology to discuss research into children's ability to conserve.
   (8 marks)

Sex and Gender

'Is it a girl or a boy?' is one of the first questions a new parent asks. The answer will affect how the baby is treated and how the child views itself. Our society has different expectations of men and women and the growing child soon learns what they are. But to what extent are these differences due to our biological make-up? This chapter first considers biological differences between males and females and then reviews some explanations for how children come to adopt the attitudes and behaviours which their society considers appropriate to their sex.

BIOLOGICAL FACTORS IN SEX DIFFERENCES

Biologically there are a number of ways in which males and females differ. These are described below.

CHROMOSOMES

The first stage in the determination of sex is the pairing of **chromosomes**. We have 23 pairs of chromosomes in each cell, one pair being the sex chromosomes. These determine the sex of the individual. In females they are XX, and in males they are XY.

During the first few weeks the foetus develops as a female. However, the Y chromosome contains genes which switches the development of the foetus into the male route. How does this happen? At about six weeks, **genes** on the Y chromosome cause the reproductive organs in the embryo to develop into **testes** (the male reproductive organs). Without the action of these genes the organs will develop into **ovaries** (the female reproductive organs). When the reproductive organs have developed in the foetus they produce **hormones**, which then take over sexual development.

HORMONES

These are the chemicals that affect the development of the internal reproductive structures and the external reproductive organs - the **genitals**. The testes in the male foetus produce **androgens**, the most important of which is **testosterone**. It is testosterone which controls development of the **penis** and **scrotum** and increases muscles, lung and heart capacity. The ovaries in the female foetus produce **oestrogen** and **progesterone** which lead to the development of the **womb** and the **vagina**. In fact both sexes produce these hormones, but in different quantities. Table 6.1 gives a summary of the biological differences between males and females.

	Females	Males
Chromosome pairing	XX	XY
Gonads (reproductive organs)	ovaries	testes
Hormones	more oestrogen and progesterone	more androgens (including testosterone)
Genitalia (external sex organs)	clitoris and vagina	penis and scrotum

Table 6.1 *Summary of the biological differences between males and females*

For most individuals all the above features correspond, for instance a boy will have the XY chromosome pairing, testes, higher levels of androgens, a penis and scrotum. However, sometimes disorders occur, for example a male foetus may produce testosterone but his body does not respond to it. As a result, male characteristics do not develop.

SEX AND GENDER

The words 'sex' and 'gender' are sometimes used as though they mean the same thing, and on other occasions as though they have different meanings. They do have different meanings, as you can see:

- **Sex** refers to biological aspects of the individual, such as those described above. For example, a child's sex is identified at birth by its genitals.
- **Gender** refers to the psychological and cultural aspects of maleness or femaleness.

SEX IDENTITY AND GENDER IDENTITY

Sex identity is the biological status of being male or female. As we saw above, in most individuals the four indicators of sex which are listed in Table 6.1 correspond to the individual's sexual identity. The genitals are the usual indicators of the sex of a newborn infant because they are visible, and it is from this point that the child's development is influenced by its experiences.

These experiences contribute to our **gender identity**, our sense of being male or being female. Some adults whose sex identity is male say they feel as though they are female; we say their gender identity is female. So gender identity refers to the individual's feelings of being either male or female. These experiences are linked to the expectations every society has about its members, about what behaviours, characteristics, attitudes, jobs and so on are appropriate for males and for females. These expectations are called **gender roles**.

Understanding Psychology

Below we examine two explanations for how the developing child comes to adopt the behaviours and attitudes which society sees as appropriate to its sex – how its gender identity develops.

THE PSYCHOANALYTIC EXPLANATION FOR GENDER ACQUISITION

Freud proposed that instinctive drives underlie human behaviour. The way we cope with one of these drives – the **libido** – explains how gender identity develops. At about four years of age a child's libido becomes focused on the genitals: this generates a desire for the opposite-sex parent. However, the child also fears that the same-sex parent will be very angry when this desire is discovered. This creates anxiety in the child, which is resolved as follows:

- A boy experiences the **Oedipus conflict** because of his desire for his mother and fear that his father will castrate him. To resolve this conflict (to reduce anxiety) the boy identifies with his father – he adopts his father's behaviours, speech and attitudes. This reduces the threat from his father and brings the boy closer to his mother. Through **identification** with his father, the boy internalises male character-istics and acquires his **male identity**.

Figure 6.1 *According to Freud, this boy has identified with his father and is adopting his behaviours*

- A girl experiences the **Electra conflict**: she has unconscious longings for her father, experiencing penis envy, yet fears loss of her mother's love. Because she thinks she has already been castrated by her mother, she is not so fearful of her as the boy is of his father. Her **identification** with her mother, in order to reduce the conflict, is therefore less strong than that of the boy. Nevertheless she adopts and internalises the characteristics of her mother and so acquires her **female identity.**

These feelings, and the way they are resolved, all take place in the child's unconscious. Freud called this the **phallic** stage of psychosexual development, and it is completed by the age of about six years old.

Evidence for Freud's explanation comes from his study of Little Hans, a five-year-old whose parents followed Freud's ideas. The boy had been very frightened when he saw a horse fall in the street. He thought it was dead. Subsequently he developed a fear of horses; he feared they would bite him and that they would fall down.

Over several months the boy's father wrote to Freud, describing incidents and conversations which seemed to be related to his fear. Freud interpreted this information in terms of the principles described above, noting evidence of the boy's sexual longings for his mother. Freud proposed that the horse represented the child's father, who Hans wished would leave or die. Hans was also frightened that his penis would be cut off, and, according to Freud, this was linked to his fear of being bitten by the horse. Finally, Hans told his father that he imagined he was given a much larger penis and agreed with his father's suggestion that he wanted to be like his father.

CRITICAL APPRAISAL

There are several criticisms of the psychoanalytic explanation. Some of the main ones are that:

- Children much younger than four years old have some understanding of gender identity, such as preferring gender-typed toys and activities.
- Freud's theory was based on a few **case studies** of his female patients who all came from a similar background, so his sample was not representative of people in general. He did not study children directly, yet much of his theory is based on childhood experiences.
- It is extremely difficult to test his theory scientifically because he uses concepts such as 'libido' and 'identification' which are not directly observable and measurable. If these conflicts are in the unconscious as Freud described, then they are not accessible for studying and testing.
- Freud's explanation ignores biological and social influences on gender development.

PRACTICAL IMPLICATIONS

Freud's view is that gender identity is rooted in an unconscious conflict between two innate drives, the resolution of which leads to the development of gender identity. From this view, the child must have a parent of each sex for gender identity to develop properly.

This means that children raised in one-parent, lesbian or homosexual families will have difficulties in developing their gender identity. This would have implications for social services and adoption agencies, who must make decisions about 'suitable' families for children in their care. However, several studies have compared children raised in one-parent, two-parent, lesbian and homosexual homes and found no evidence of problems with gender identity.

THE SOCIAL LEARNING EXPLANATION FOR GENDER ACQUISITION

According to social learning theory a girl learns what it means to be a girl, and a boy what it means to be a boy, through observation, imitation and reinforcement.

OBSERVATION

Children notice what other people do and how they do it, what they say and how they say it. They notice how other people respond to what is said or done, so they observe the consequences of other people's behaviour. As a result of this **observation**, the child may then **imitate**, or copy, the behaviour. These are the principles established by Albert Bandura, largely as a result of his research on aggression.

IMITATION

Anyone whose behaviour is observed like this is called a **model**, and children are more likely to imitate the behaviour of models who are:

- **Similar** – such as someone of the same sex. The results of Bandura's research on aggression showed that children produced twice as many acts of imitative aggression when they had seen aggression performed by a same-sex model than when an opposite-sex model had performed the aggressive act (for details, see Table 9.1, p. 99). They learn what is appropriate for their sex by noting how often a behaviour is performed by others of the same sex. This indicates to them what is typical of their own sex, as well as of the other sex. As Bandura noted, when a boy saw a woman kick the Bobo doll, he commented 'ladies shouldn't do things like that' (p. 99).
- **Reinforced** – if the child sees that the model's behaviour leads to pleasant consequences (such as gaining approval), this is called **vicarious reinforcement** because the child is reinforced indirectly. So a boy who sees a man congratulated for his bravery is more likely to observe and remember his actions.

The child may later imitate the model's behaviour, which may be one reason why children enjoy toys or activities related to their sex, for instance girls like make-up because they see women using it, and boys prefer playing football because that is what men do.

REINFORCEMENT

In accordance with the principles of **operant conditioning**, if a behaviour is rewarded it is more likely to be repeated. So if a little girl puts make-up on and is then told 'What a pretty lady you are', she is more likely to repeat the behaviour. Beverly Fagot (1978) carried out **naturalistic observations** of the interactions between parents and their two-year-old children. She found that the girls were rewarded for playing with dolls and helping, whereas boys were rewarded for being independent and active in their play. Parents encouraged boys to climb, but disapproved when their daughters did so. These results show that parents treat their children differently and encourage them in gender-related activities. According to the principles of operant conditioning, behaviour which is not appropriate will be weakened if it is ignored or frowned upon. These consequences are examples of punishment.

CRITICAL APPRAISAL

Social learning theory proposes that the child acquires its gender identity through observation and imitation of models and reinforcement of behaviour which is considered appropriate to the child's sex. However, Karen Bussey and Albert Bandura (1984) have proposed that gender-typed behaviour is initially shaped by the responses of others, but as the child gets older he constructs his own personal gender identity. He will, for example, begin to note what seems to be appropriate behaviour for each sex.

The social learning approach fails to take account of the biological differences we reviewed at the start of this chapter. It focuses on social factors, which do seem to be important. However, the social learning approach is unable to explain why:

- Children prefer sex-typed toys and activities by about two years of age. Observational learning and reinforcement are, by themselves, unlikely to produce such strong preferences at such a young age.
- Children reared in one-parent or homosexual families do not have difficulties with the development of gender identity. There is no evidence that the absence of a powerful same-sex model, or non-stereotypical models for male or female behaviour, affect a child's gender identity.
- Children persist in behaviour which they do not see modelled. The film *Billy Elliott* is an example of this. Billy was drawn to ballet and desperately wanted to be a ballet dancer, despite being surrounded by men who were typical of the male **stereotype**. The only ballet dancers he saw were female, but he did not want to be female, he was comfortable as a male. He just wanted to dance.

Figure 6.2 *A still from* Billy Elliott

PRACTICAL IMPLICATIONS

The implications of the social learning approach are that gender is constructed by the society we live in. If we were brought up in a society with different expectations and behaviours for males and females, perhaps one where the distinction between male and female did not exist, then **gender identity** would have no meaning. If we look at how gender differences are promoted and reinforced, this point may become clearer.

SOCIAL INFLUENCES ON GENDER DIFFERENCES

From the moment of birth the label girl/boy becomes a key element of our self-concept, our knowledge of the kind of person we are and how we fit into our society. We will look at some of the ways in which society differentiates us on the basis of sex and what our society's expectations are – the **gender stereotypes** which are held.

GENDER STEREOTYPES

Deborah Best and her colleagues (1977) reported that children in America, England and Ireland (all around nine years old) held the following stereotypes:

- **men** – strong, robust, aggressive, cruel, coarse, ambitious, dominant
- **women** – weak, emotional, soft-hearted, sentimental, sophisticated, affectionate.

In later research, John Williams and Deborah Best (1994) asked people from several cultures about male and female characteristics. The results showed that these were similar to the characteristics provided by the children, for example men were aggressive, determined and sharp-witted whilst women were emotional, cautious and warm. Others have summarised the stereotypical characteristics as 'hard' and 'soft'.

Research also indicates that children develop stereotypes for males at a younger age than those for females. The male stereotype is also stronger – children are more likely to agree on male attributes than female attributes.

Some of the most powerful influences on the promotion and reinforcement of gender differences are the family, the media and school. The discussion below illustrates the principles of **operant conditioning** and social learning theory.

THE FAMILY

Jeffrey Rubin and his colleagues (1977) found that parents expect gender differences because, within 24 hours of their baby's birth, parents of girls described their daughters as softer and smaller than boys, whereas parents of boys thought their sons were more alert, stronger and better co-ordinated. Fathers tended to see greater differences between the sexes than did mothers, although there was no apparent physical difference between the male and female infants. This research shows that parents already stereotype their infants before any stereotypical behaviour is evident.

In another study, observations of experienced mothers interacting with a 'stranger' baby revealed that when the baby was dressed as a boy it was handled more vigorously and given toys such as a hammer-shaped rattle. When the same baby was dressed as a girl it was held and talked to more and given soft toys to play with. So parents may be stereotyping the baby, treating it in accordance with its sex. Parents continue to convey their expectations of these differences as the child gets older, perhaps by providing toys which enable their children to imitate the behaviour of same-sex models.

Research indicates that fathers are more concerned than mothers that children show appropriate behaviour, particularly their sons. They encourage them to be active and independent but discourage them from showing weakness and taking part in 'girls' activities. However, they are less troubled if girls play 'tomboy' games.

A study by Robert Sears and his colleagues (1977) investigated parenting style and aggression (see p. 104 for details). The results showed that parents tolerated aggression in their sons much more than in their daughters, and parents were more likely to punish a boy if he hit a girl than if he hit another boy.

What if parents do not promote or reinforce gender differences? A study of six-year-olds whose parents tried to treat them the same, regardless of their sex, shows that they were not much different from conventionally reared children in their choice of friends and play activities. However, they did hold less **stereotyped** beliefs. This suggests parental influence on their understanding may be stronger than on their behaviour.

Figure 6.3 *These toys encourage the child to adopt sex-typed behaviour*

THE MEDIA

The media includes television, films, newspapers, magazines, radio, books, computer programs and the Internet. They are influential because they provide models for **observational learning**, as well as information relating to stereotypes. When stereotyping occurs in the media it promotes differences between males and females. In addition, these differences are reinforced when models are rewarded for sex-typed behaviour.

Stereotyping in the media was investigated by Antony Manstead and Caroline McCulloch (1981) using the **content analysis technique**. They analysed all advertisements transmitted by a TV channel over seven evenings, except for repeats and those portraying only children or fantasy characters. The total sample was 170. They noted the central figures in terms of various characteristics, such as role, whether they were product users or authorities on the product and reasons for using the product.

The results showed that 70 per cent of the figures seen to give authoritative information about products were male but 65 per cent of product users were females; females appeared much more frequently in dependent roles and men in autonomous roles; 64 per cent of figures seen at work were males, whereas 73 per cent of figures seen at home were females; females were more likely to use a product for reasons of social approval or self-enhancement.

To summarise, the males were more likely to be portrayed as authoritative, workers, independent, active and females as dependent, home-based, consumers, passive. We can conclude that these advertisements portrayed males and females in gender roles which were stereotypical for the period.

Figure 6.4 *This ad illustrates the female stereotype, as described above*

In children's fairy stories (Snow White, Sleeping Beauty, Cinderella) there are beautiful helpless heroines who are rescued by strong adventurous princes. History books are filled with males who are heroes, kings, explorers, adventurers, scientists – with little mention of women. In computer games and cartoons males perform 'action' roles; even where women take the lead they are always beautiful.

These stereotypes not only provide information on what men and women do, but they also imply what is appropriate for males and females. This relates to the point made by Bussey and Bandura (1984) (p. 65) – children infer what is appropriate from what they see around them.

Are children aware of the **gender differences** being promoted? Aletha Huston (1984) noted that adverts for boys' toys were loud and fast, whereas those for girls' toys were soft and fuzzy. When six-year-olds were shown adverts for a 'neutral' toy, but in either the 'fast' or the 'fuzzy' style, they could tell whether it was aimed at a girl or a boy by the style it used.

Terry Frueh and Paul McGhee (1975) investigated the amount of television children watched and how stereotypical were their ideas. Their results showed that children who watched a lot of television had fairly stereotypical ideas and those who watched little television had less stereotypical ideas.

CORRELATIONAL STUDY

In a correlational study the psychologist calculates whether there is a relationship between two variables. What are the two variables in Frueh and McGhee's (1975) study? Did they find a positive or negative correlation? What cannot be concluded from these results? For help in answering these questions, see p. 153.

In defence of the influence of the media, critics point out that:

- children are active in selecting information and developing their own understanding, so evidence that children can differentiate between adverts does not necessarily mean that they accept the images projected
- everyday experiences with family, school and friends provide children with information which may not conform to stereotypes
- the media also provides non-stereotypical information; the characters in children's books are less stereotyped; increasingly women are seen in positions of authority and responsibility and they do perform non-stereotypical roles in TV programmes.

AT SCHOOL

School is an important social setting for children. It gives them opportunities to negotiate relationships with others: peers and teachers provide **models** and **reinforcement** (or **punishment**) for behaviour. Ways in which gender differences can be promoted and reinforced in the school environment include:

- Peers provide reinforcement and punishment – boys make fun of another boy when he does not conform to 'boy' behaviour, perhaps imitating the behaviour of their fathers. Beverly Fagot (1985) found that nursery school teachers rewarded boys and girls for stereotypically female behaviour such as playing quietly. However, boys tended to continue their stereotypically male behaviour (such as noisy play). Their behaviour did not change until other boys showed approval or disapproval. These results show that a boy's peers may have more influence than a teacher.
- If children are separated on the basis of gender – 'boys line up here and girls over there' – or are discouraged from studying certain subjects at school, this promotes gender differences.

- Observational studies indicate that teachers treat children differently according to sex – they spend more time talking to boys than girls. This seems to be partly because boys are more disruptive in class, but also teachers reward boys for trying but girls for being well-behaved.
- The **role models** which teachers provide are also influential. The majority of primary teachers are female, yet a greater proportion of headteachers are male. In secondary schools there are more males than females teaching science and maths and holding senior positions. This tells children what sorts of jobs males and females do and who is more likely to hold the positions of power.

THE IMPLICATIONS FOR EVERYDAY LIFE

We started this chapter by looking at the biological differences between males and females, and have ended by considering ways in which gender differences and stereotypes may be established and reinforced. Having said this, there appear to be very few distinct gender differences, according to Eleanor Maccoby and Carol Jacklin's 1974 survey of more than 1,500 studies. In addition, they point out that research which does not indicate differences is less likely to be published than that which does, thus creating a biased impression of actual differences.

The role of the media is important in promoting and reinforcing stereotypes and in doing so, it says stereotyping is acceptable. This may be one of the reasons stereotyping and discrimination continue. Women tend to be discriminated against when applying for managerial positions, according to R. Reilly and G. Chao (1982). It may be more difficult for men to be accepted in work with children or with older people.

According to the principles of equal opportunities, society should not focus on what males and females can and cannot do, but should ensure that they have equal access to education, training and experiences so that each person may fulfil their own potential.

Sample Exam Questions

1 What do psychologists mean by 'gender identity'?
   (2 marks)

2 Describe the role of hormones in sexual development.
   (4 marks)

3 In psychoanalytic theory, what is meant by the term 'identification'?
   (2 marks)

4 Use your knowledge of psychology to outline the social learning explanation of how children develop gender identity.
   (6 marks)

5 Describe one study which has investigated the role of the media in the promotion of gender differences.
   (4 marks)

6 Discuss the influence of the family in promoting and reinforcing gender differences.
   (6 marks)

CHAPTER 7

The Development of Moral Behaviour

Morality refers to what we consider to be fair or unfair, good or bad, right or wrong. Everyone has their own ideas, but these generally reflect the moral standards of their culture. Our moral behaviour is not always in accord with our moral standards, however. You know it is wrong to cheat in an exam and would not do it, but if someone's answer paper slipped onto the floor next to you, would you look?

MORAL BEHAVIOUR

Moral behaviour is the way we conduct ourselves in relation to our moral standards. Cheating in an exam is the behaviour, but if I asked you why it was wrong, then you would refer to your moral standards. You might say that the cheat is gaining an unfair advantage over other candidates, or that they would be punished if they were found out. Your answer shows your moral reasoning. How does this sense of right and wrong develop? We will now examine four approaches to moral development.

THE BEHAVIOURIST APPROACH

Details of the **behaviourist** approach are given in Chapter 11, but it is based on the principle that behaviour is shaped and maintained by its consequences. Therefore moral behaviour is learned through **reinforcement** of acceptable responses. If a child shares a toy with another child and receives a smile of approval from an adult, the child is likely to repeat the behaviour.

Negative reinforcement also strengthens moral behaviour. If a boy sees another child who is upset he may experience distress. This distress is unpleasant, and one way to relieve it is to make the other child stop crying. If the boy offers a toy or a sweet to the child who is crying, and the crying stops, the boy's own distress is reduced. This is an example of negative reinforcement, because offering comfort has stopped an unpleasant experience. Thus in the future the boy is more likely to offer comfort to others.

Punishment should weaken behaviour, but research by Martin Hoffman (1970) suggests it is not as effective as reinforcement and explanation. Hoffman investigated the relationship between a child's moral behaviour and the way the parent used discipline. He asked children, their classmates and their parents a variety of questions relating to helpful behaviour and to discipline. From the results he proposed three types of discipline:

- **Inductive discipline,** which meant reasoning with the child, encouraging the child to think about its behaviour, the consequences and how his or her parents felt. This encourages empathy for others and a sense of personal responsibility for one's actions.
- **Power assertive discipline,** where the parent used threats or force, or withdrew privileges. Hoffman suggested this style creates hostility and anger.
- **Love withdrawal,** which involved ignoring or isolating the child, thus creating anxiety.

From his results, Hoffman concluded that there were two types of moral behaviour related to these styles of discipline. **Internalised moral behaviour** is shown by children who behave morally even when there is no external pressure to do so. This behaviour is related to the inductive, and to a lesser degree the love withdrawal style.

Externalised moral behaviour is shown by children who behave morally in order to avoid punishment. They tend to show less concern about others and this behaviour is related to the power assertive style of parental discipline.

CRITICAL EVALUATION

Children do seem to be inconsistent in their moral behaviour, which is explained by the behaviourists as being due to different patterns of reinforcement. For example, a child may be helpful at school because she is given a star but she is not helpful at home because her helpfulness is not rewarded. Nevertheless, there are a number of important criticisms of the behaviourist approach, such as:

- The effectiveness of reinforcement varies enormously, for instance some children do continue to behave unkindly and selfishly even when they are rewarded for the right kind of behaviour.
- Punishment is not very effective; it does not show what behaviour is desirable. It can create frustration and anger (which may lead to more immoral behaviour) and the person providing the punishment is giving the child a model for how to get your own way – by punishment. Yet research suggests that adults often punish wrong behaviour but rarely reward correct moral behaviour.
- Research indicates that although moral behaviour is inconsistent, there are nevertheless some consistent patterns in moral development which this approach cannot explain. Evidence for these patterns is given later in the section on the Cognitive Approach (pp. 74–77).
- The behaviourist approach provides a possible explanation of how behaviour develops but fails to explain how moral thinking develops.

THE SOCIAL LEARNING APPROACH

Social learning theory proposes that moral development occurs as a result of a child **observing** and **imitating** the behaviour of significant others (as outlined in Chapter 11). For instance, children learn moral behaviour by observing and imitating a parent who donates to charity, or an older brother when he unpacks the shopping. Children are also more likely to imitate models whose behaviour is **reinforced**, like the child's mother in Figure 7.1, who is being rewarded by the big smile of the person collecting money.

Figure 7.1 *This model may affect the child's moral development*

If a child imitates behaviour and is then reinforced, she is more likely to continue the behaviour, so it is through these processes of observation, imitation and reinforcement that the child learns how to behave in a moral way. These behaviours gradually become internalised, and the child generates appropriate behaviour without it being modelled. Albert Bandura (1977) called this **self-efficacy**, which is the feeling of competence in and appropriateness of our behaviour and abilities. Behaving in accordance with these internalised standards is rewarding; it increases our self-efficacy.

Television can encourage moral behaviour by providing models who behave prosocially. This was investigated in a study of five- and six-year-olds by L. Friedrich and A. Stein (1973). The children watched a television programme over four days; the **experimental** group watched a pro-social one and the **control** group watched a neutral programme.

> **HYPOTHESIS, INDEPENDENT AND DEPENDENT VARIABLES**
> In Chapter 13 there are details of how to write a hypothesis, and what we mean by the independent variable (IV) and the dependent variable (DV). Use this information to write a hypothesis for Friedrich and Stein's (1973) research. What is the IV? What is the DV?

The results showed that the children in the experimental group showed more understanding and behaviour which was pro-social, especially if they were first encouraged to role-play what they had seen in the programme. We can conclude that children's moral development can be increased if they observe helping behaviour and are reinforced when they imitate that behaviour.

CRITICAL EVALUATION

Social learning theory explains why children may show moral behaviour in one situation and not in another, because the behaviour can depend on someone providing rewards. It also highlights the importance of significant others in a child's moral development. However, critics point out that:

- It is based on research which is artificial, for example experiments have used films of adults modelling behaviour which children watch. This is not like real life, where children may have distractions or may interact with the models.
- This approach predicts that children will learn moral behaviour as a direct result of what they experience, therefore there will not be a consistent pattern in children's moral development. Research shows that there is a consistent pattern, as we will see now under the cognitive approach.

THE COGNITIVE APPROACH TO MORAL DEVELOPMENT

This approach views children's moral development as being dependent on their **cognitive development**. Cognitive development follows a consistent pattern, and so does moral development (although the pattern occurs a little later). You will notice that the two explanations we are going to examine focus on what a child says, which is taken as evidence of the child's understanding and thinking about moral behaviour.

PIAGET'S THEORY OF MORAL DEVELOPMENT

As part of his research on cognitive development (see Chapter 5), Jean Piaget studied children's moral development. He played games of marbles with children whilst asking them questions about the rules they created, and what would happen if the rules were broken, or did not work very well.

Another method was to ask questions about the behaviour of children in stories. For instance in one story a boy breaks a cup whilst stealing some jam, and another boy breaks lots of cups by accident. Piaget then asked the child 'Which boy was the naughtiest? Which boy should be punished more? Why?'

The results showed that children under about eight years of age said the boy who broke all the cups was the naughtiest, so he should be punished more. These children were making moral judgements on the basis of the consequences of a person's actions. By eight years old, children were able to make the correct judgement because they took the person's intent into account as well. They were able to decentre (see p. 54).

From research such as this, Piaget (1932) concluded that up to the age of about three or four a child is unable to make moral judgements because she does not understand rules, so she cannot understand breaking rules. Once she understands rules her moral development starts. Piaget proposed that this occurs in two stages:

- Stage 1 – **Heteronomous morality** (morality imposed from outside). The child sees rules as being made by parents, teachers and God, and they are unchangeable. Moral judgements are based on rules – if you do something wrong you will be punished. The child is at the **pre-operational stage** of development, so she can attend to only one aspect of a situation (see p. 51). In Piaget's story the child attends to the most vivid aspect – the consequences of the action, so the child who breaks the most cups is judged to be the naughtiest.
- Stage 2 – **Autonomous morality** (morality based on your own rules). This appears when the child is able to **decentre**, so she can judge the intent behind the action as well as the consequence. Children now understand that rules can be flexible to suit the situation; they make up their own rules and take account of other people's perspective. For instance, when playing hide and seek, a young child will be allowed to count to a lower number. Piaget argued that because males play in larger groups than females, this opportunity to take account of others' views and negotiate rules leads to higher levels of moral reasoning in males.

CRITICAL EVALUATION OF PIAGET'S THEORY
Although children's moral development does seem to follow this general pattern, there have been criticisms of Piaget's theory, for example:

- Research has shown that when the intention is emphasised, even three-year-olds can make the correct judgements. This echoes criticism that Piaget's theory of cognitive development underestimates children's cognitive abilties (see pp. 52–55).
- There is no evidence to show that girls have weaker moral development than boys; if anything it seems to be stronger.
- Despite evidence which generally supports this pattern of moral development, we do not always behave in accordance with our knowledge of what is right or wrong.
- The stages are too general and suggest there is no significant change in moral thinking beyond early adolescence, although research suggests that there is. This research is described in the next cognitive–developmental explanation.

KOHLBERG'S THEORY OF MORAL DEVELOPMENT

Lawrence Kohlberg's theory identifies more stages in the developmental process, and continues it into adulthood. Kohlberg (1967) wanted to investigate people's moral reasoning, so he told them a story – a moral dilemma – and then asked them questions. One of his best-known moral dilemmas is the story of Heinz, as described in Figure 7.2.

HEINZ' DILEMMA

Heinz' wife was dying of cancer. Doctors said a new drug might save her. The drug had been discovered by a pharmacist in Heinz' town but he was charging a lot of money for it – 10 times what it cost him to make. Heinz couldn't afford to buy the drug, so he asked friends and relatives to lend him money. But still he only had half the money he needed. He told the pharmacist his wife was dying and asked him to sell the drug cheaper, or asked if he could pay the rest of the money later. The pharmacist said no, he had discovered the drug and was going to make money on it. Heinz got desperate so he broke in to the pharmacy and stole some of the drug.

Sample of questions:

1 Should Heinz have stolen the drug?
2 Would it change anything if Heinz did not love his wife?
3 What if the person dying was a stranger, would it make any difference?

Figure 7.2 *Heinz' dilemma and some questions about it*

Kohlberg posed dilemmas such as this to a sample of 84 boys over a 20-year period. Having analysed the answers, Kohlberg (1969) proposed that there were three levels of moral reasoning, each having two stages.

- Level 1 – Pre-conventional morality (authority is outside the individual and reasoning is based on the physical consequences of actions). The first stage relates to punishment of actions – if it is punished it must have been wrong. People who have greater power are obeyed. The second stage is determined by behaviour which brings personal gain such as a reward, or help from someone else – 'the pharmacist should have let Heinz pay later, because one day he might need something from Heinz'.
- Level 2 – Conventional morality (authority is internalised but not questioned and reasoning is based on the norms of the group to which the person belongs). At the first stage answers are related to the approval of others; saying that people like you when you do good, helpful things. The second stage reasoning is based on respect for law and order – not the authority of specific people like parents, but a generalised social norm of obedience to authority and doing one's duty.
- Level 3 – Post-conventional morality (individual judgement is based on self-chosen principles, and moral reasoning is based on individual rights and justice). Reasoning at the first stage says that although laws are important, to be fair there are times when they must be changed or ignored. For example, in Heinz' dilemma the protection of life is more important than breaking the law against stealing. In the second stage people assume personal responsiblity for their actions, based on

universal ethical and moral principles which are not necessarily laid down by society. Kohlberg doubted few ever reached this stage.

Kohlberg proposed that these three levels of moral reasoning are universal. He did not tie the levels to a specific age, although research has suggested that Level 1 is up to about ten years old, Level 2 is ten years up to adulthood, and very few adults show Level 3 reasoning. He found that generally males achieved higher levels of moral reasoning than females.

CRITICAL EVALUATION OF KOHLBERG'S THEORY

Kohlberg's theory does provide more detail than Piaget's and reflects changing levels of morality in adulthood. Research shows that the changes in moral reasoning that Kohlberg identified do occur in this order. However the theory has been criticised on a number of points, for example:

- It is very difficult for participants to put their reasoning into words, particularly when they include abstract ideas of justice, so they may have moral understanding relating to the higher levels but be unable to express it.
- As in the criticism of Piaget, the cognitive approach stresses thinking and reasoning rather than behaviour and we do not always behave in accordance with our knowledge of what is right or wrong.
- Kohlberg's theory is ethnocentric; he viewed morality from the viewpoint of his own (Western) society. Other cultures have different values which would lead to different types of reasoning and judgements on moral dilemmas.
- In his research, the dilemmas were faced by males and most of his participants were male, which led to biased results. Carol Gilligan's (1982) research, which is described on page 81, addresses this point.
- There is no evidence to show that girls have weaker moral development than boys; if anything it seems to be stronger.

THE PSYCHOANALYTIC APPROACH

An example of the psychoanalytic approach is Freud's theory, in which he proposed that the moral part of the personality is the **superego**. This develops as a result of a child's **identification** with the same-sex parent during the **phallic stage** of **psycho-sexual development**, which is explained in Chapter 6, Sex and Gender (p. 62).

Through identification with his father, a boy adopts his father's moral standards. Because a girl's identification with her mother is less strong, Freud claimed that she will have a weaker moral sense than the boy. Freud predicts, therefore, that once a child has identified with the same-sex parent (which has happened by about seven years of age), the child is morally mature.

This 'internal parent' is represented by the part of the personality called the superego, according to Freud. The superego comprises:

- **the ego-ideal**, which represents the kind of person the child wants to be – it is the rewarding and approving parent; the source of pride when we do the right thing
- **the conscience**, which watches the child's behaviour and stops it from doing the wrong thing; it is the punishing parent, the source of guilt when we do the wrong thing.

According to this theory, we would expect to feel guilty when we do something we know to be wrong. However, Freud predicted the opposite, because he argued that when the conscience stops us from satisfying our basic impulses, the energy which drives them is available to the conscience, and is directed inwards towards ourselves. We experience this as guilt. As a result, those with the strongest consciences will experience the greatest guilt and have the highest moral behaviour.

This was investigated by D. MacKinnon (1938) who gave participants problems to solve whilst alone in a room with answer books. He found that approximately 50 per cent of participants cheated, although they did not know they had been found out. Several participants showed frustration whilst doing the task, such as swearing, and kicking or pounding the table.

A month later he asked these participants whether they had cheated and about half of them confessed. He then asked about feeling guilty and asked some of the male participants about the type of punishment they had received as children. A summary of the results is shown in Table 7.1.

	Cheats	Non-Cheats
I did/would feel guilty about cheating	25%	84%
In everyday life I often feel guilty	29%	75%
Behaviour when solving problems (swearing, pounding fists)	31%	4%
Type of punishment received – physical	78%	48%
– psychological	22%	52%

Table 7.1 *Results of MacKinnon's study of cheating and guilt*

These results support Freud's claim that those demonstrating the higher moral behaviour will also experience more guilt. His explanation, which is that this is because of the unused energy from the instincts we have not expressed, is also supported because those who seemed to be releasing their pent-up aggression were the ones who experienced less guilt. Finally, more of the cheats experienced physical punishment than the non-cheats.

CRITICAL EVALUATION

Freud's theory can explain some of the research evidence. This is more convincing when the moral behaviour is not what we might expect, as we have seen above. There are a number of aspects of moral behaviour which remain unexplained, however, as well as criticisms of the psychoanalytic approach in general. These include:

- Moral development does not occur only during the phallic stage. This chapter notes that children younger than five years of age show knowledge of right and wrong and children are not morally mature by seven years old. Moral development continues well beyond this age, as Kohlberg (p. 75) and Eisenberg (p. 80) showed.

- As noted in regard to the cognitive explanations, research suggests that girls' moral development is actually more advanced than that of boys, in contrast to what Freud claimed.
- Children who are reared in single-parent families should have poor moral development as they do not experience conflicts at the phallic stage which lead to identification with the same-sex parent, yet research has failed to find this.
- Freud devised his theory when family influences were very strong, but nowadays there are many other influences on a child's moral development, such as other adults, school friends and the media.
- Since Freud, other psychoanalysts have stressed the importance of the ego in the individual's moral development, rather than instincts as Freud did. They say that the development of the ego (or self) takes place over many years, and depends not only on parents but also on 'significant others' such as teachers or peers.

Figure 7.3 *Which of the four approaches considered in this chapter provide the best explanation for why this child cares for his little brother like this?*

RESEARCH ON MORAL DEVELOPMENT

We have considered four approaches to moral development and noted some of the strengths and weaknesses of each. However, there has been criticism of the research on which some of these approaches are based. As you will see, these critics have conducted their own research, which has given a different view of moral development.

SIEGEL AND STOREY'S RESEARCH

Although psychoanalytic and cognitive–developmental explanations consider that moral development does not occur until five or six years of age, research evidence suggests this is not so. There is also evidence that parents rarely punish children who break moral rules, but do punish them for breaking social rules. So how do children learn moral rules?

Michael Siegel and Rebecca Storey (1984) investigated whether children's moral development was the result of greater social exposure to their peers. They compared children who had attended a day-care centre for an average of two-and-a-half years with those who had only been attending for an average of three months. The children were four-and-a-quarter years of age, on average.

The children were shown pictures of 'stick' figures breaking moral rules (hitting someone else) or social rules (sitting in the wrong place at storytime). When asked to indicate how naughty the behaviour was, both groups of children thought the moral transgressions were the more serious. However, the newer children rated the social transgressions as naughtier than did the more experienced children.

DRAWING CONCLUSIONS
What conclusions can you draw from the results of the Siegel and Storey research? Try to write them down.

EISENBERG'S RESEARCH

Critics of Kohlberg claim that dilemmas (such as that of Heinz) were unrelated to the lives of most of his participants. Nancy Eisenberg's (1986) study used dilemmas which related to children's lives. She wanted to find out whether her participants would put their own interests before someone else's interests. One dilemma asks the child to imagine he is walking to a friend's birthday party but passes a child who has fallen over and is hurt. If he stays to help, he might miss the fun of the party. What should he do?

Having analysed the children's answers to these dilemmas, Eisenberg proposed six stages of **pro-social reasoning**, which are related to age:

- **Stage 1 – Self-focused** (up to six years old). The child is concerned to satisfy his own needs or to only help if the other could help him.
- **Stage 2 – Needs of others** (up to ten years old). The child shows awareness of the other child's needs.
- **Stage 3 – Approval of others** (up to 13 years old). The child behaves pro-socially because he thinks others will like him, or he should do it.
- **Stage 4 – Empathic orientation** (adolescents). Reasons for helping show empathy with others' feelings.
- **Stage 5 – Transitional** (adolescents and some adults). Reasons for helping show some evidence of acting on internalised norms or responsibilities.

- Stage 6 – **Strongly internalised** (usually seen only in adults). Reasoning shows a clear relationship between behaviour and the need to act according to one's own principles – 'I feel a personal responsibility to help'.

These six levels can be compared with Kohlberg's six stages but the child's reasoning seems more advanced. Eisenberg suggested this was because the ideas were about pro-social (or helping) behaviour, and not about what you should not do. Also, the dilemmas are easier to understand because they are related to the child's own experience.

GILLIGAN'S RESEARCH

We have noted several explanations of moral development which are biased towards males. Carol Gilligan (1982) is particularly critical of Kohlberg, arguing that he focuses on justice and fairness rather than caring for others. His classification rates justice more highly than caring because he studied mostly males. Gilligan argues that females are more concerned about caring and responsibility for others because they are socialised into an ethic of caring. She investigated the responses which females gave to real-life dilemmas, and from the results she concluded that women go through three stages of pro-social reasoning:

- caring for self
- caring for others
- balancing the requirements of care for self with care for others.

She also concluded that females and males show similar levels of pro-social reasoning, which is supported by other research. However, she did find a difference in the emphasis, namely that the pro-social reasoning of females is based on caring rather than justice.

Sample Exam Questions

1 **Explain how reinforcement might contribute to moral behaviour.**
   (2 marks)

2 **Describe one of Piaget's stages of moral development.**
   (2 marks)

3 **Describe and evaluate one study conducted by a cognitive psychologist in which moral behaviour was investigated.**
   (8 marks)

4 **Describe the social learning explanation of moral development.**
   (4 marks)

5 **Outline two criticisms of the psychoanalytic approach to moral development.**
   (4 marks)

6 **Using your knowledge of psychology, discuss the behaviourist approach to moral development.**
   (8 marks)

Pro-social Behaviour

In this chapter we are going to look at behaviour which helps other people – a student who offers to share revision with a classmate, a little boy who tries to comfort his crying sister, a teenager who gives up her seat on a bus to an older person or someone who dives into the sea to rescue a drowning child. These are all examples of pro-social behaviour. Helping others often causes us inconvenience, requires time and perhaps risk to ourselves, so why do we do it? This chapter suggests some of the reasons.

PRO-SOCIAL BEHAVIOUR

Pro-social behaviour can be defined as any behaviour which helps other people. As we see later in this chapter, there are **social norms** about helping others, but **altruism** is helping another willingly, without expectation of reward or pressure from anyone else. It is done without thought of one's own well-being, indeed it may involve personal cost such as time, effort, safety or expense.

Figure 8.1 These people are showing altruistic behaviour, according to the definition above

EMPATHY

We have noted that there may be considerable costs if we behave altruistically, so why do we do it? One explanation is that we feel empathy for the other person, and this makes us act. **Empathy** can be defined as the ability to match one's own feelings with those of another person. There is disagreement as to whether the emotions have to be identical to the other's, or just similar. Research by C. Daniel Batson (1983) showed that participants who were high in empathy preferred to take on someone else's suffering rather than watch them suffer. See page 90 for details of this research.

Martin Hoffman (1982) proposed that the development of empathy is linked to cognitive development and that it occurs in four stages.

STAGE 1: GLOBAL EMPATHY

During the first year of life an infant shows empathy through its behaviour, such as crying when it hears another baby crying. This could be because the infant is still **egocentric**, and therefore is unable to distinguish between itself and others. Hoffman says this empathic response is due either to inborn human tendencies towards empathy or to early **classical conditioning**.

According to classical conditioning principles, the empathic response is created by association. When a baby is hurt it feels pain, it cries, it may see blood. In other words it feels distress. As these experiences are repeated it learns to associate a cry of pain, or the sight of blood, with a feeling of distress. Because of this association, it will come to feel distress when it hears others cry, or when it sees blood.

In Figure 8.2 you can see that the baby's unhappy expression is imitated by the mother. She is comforting the child by showing she knows his feelings, in other words she is showing empathy. This baby is not aware of what he looks like, but he is learning from his mother that his feelings of unhappiness are associated with this particular expression. In classical conditioning terms, seeing this expression in others will automatically trigger his feelings of unhappiness.

Figure 8.2 Giving comfort and encouraging empathy

STAGE 2: EGOCENTRIC EMPATHY

From about one year old, toddlers respond to the feelings of others, so they will try to comfort a crying child, or show fear when another child is frightened. However, because they are still egocentric they will try to relieve the other's distress by doing something which they themselves would find comforting. For example, a toddler may offer a favourite toy to her mother who has a cut finger. The child is showing an empathic response but is not able to understand how to relieve the other's distress.

STAGE 3: EMPATHY FOR ANOTHER'S FEELINGS

From two years of age children start to show they can identify others' feelings, and respond in the appropriate way. They may try to mend a broken toy, or wipe up spilled juice. As egocentricity reduces, the child is increasingly able to take the perspective of someone else – which is sometimes called role-taking. Research has shown that there is a positive correlation between role-taking and helping behaviour. However this is only apparent from about seven years or older, when role-taking has started to develop.

At this age children will not simply respond to what they see, they can also make inferences. They know why Mum will be more unhappy when she tears a favourite dress than when she tears a tea-towel. As they get older they may show a real effort to understand the other's emotions in order to relieve the other's distress.

STAGE 4: EMPATHY FOR ANOTHER'S GENERAL PLIGHT

From about ten years of age children begin to recognise the implications of someone else's situation – poverty, for example, as well as immediate distress. They may also understand the plight of large groups of people, such as victims of war, famine or earthquakes. This is possible because the child has developed the ability to understand other people's experiences, so for example they know that people do not always show the emotions they feel. By the time the child has reached late adolescence, empathy should have developed fully.

FACTORS AFFECTING PRO-SOCIAL BEHAVIOUR

Below we consider two groups of factors which affect pro-social behaviour; those related to **social norms** and those related to **socialisation**.

SOCIAL NORMS

One way of explaining pro-social behaviour is to say that people do what society expects of them. These unspoken rules and expectations about how we should behave are called the **social norms**. They operate at a lower level of helping than we have looked at earlier under altruism, because these norms are about what society expects us to do, whereas altruistic behaviour is more than we would normally be expected to do. These norms exert pressure on us as to how we should behave in particular circumstances. They include the folowing:

- **Social responsibility** – we should help those who are more disadvantaged than us – like the teenager giving her seat to an older person. You might lend your notes to a fellow student who had missed classes because of illness, but not if you thought they were just lazy. If we feel a moral obligation to help then we have internalised the norm of social responsibility. We are more likely to be influenced by this norm when it does not require much effort on our part, or when the other person is not responsible for their need or obviously needs help.

- **Equality** – everyone should be treated equally, for example a teacher should give the same amount of support to every member of the class. In a family, the parent should treat all of the children the same. Most children complain at some time 'It's not fair!', which shows they understand the norm of equality at an early age.
- **Equity** – help is given in proportion to what is deserved. In contrast to the norm of equality (above), this social norm is an expectation that the teacher should help students in proportion to the amount of effort the student makes. This norm is related to 'belief in a just world', which is the idea that people get what they deserve, so the more responsible they are for the situation they are in the less help they should receive.
- **Reciprocity** – we help others when we ourselves have been helped, or expect to be helped. If you lend your class notes to a friend who misses class, you would expect her to do the same for you in the future if you asked her to. It is related to feelings of indebtedness or gratitude, and research suggests that the greater the help given, the greater the help which is returned. This emphasises that we have a sense of balance about how much help we 'owe' someone. However we are less likely to be influenced by this norm if their help required little cost or if they were forced to help us.

SOCIALISATION

Socialisation is the process by which we learn what is expected within our society – its social norms. These unwritten guidelines are learned from other members of our culture, such as parents, peers, teachers and the media. Robert Cialdini and colleagues (1981) proposed that helping behaviour in children develops in three stages:

- **Pre-socialisation stage** – the child is reluctant to help because they might have to give up something.
- **Reward stage** – they become aware of the social norms which involve rewards for helping (such as reciprocity), so they help others in order to get rewards for themselves.
- **Internalisation stage** – finally they gain satisfaction from helping others; the rewards have become internalised.

This process depends in part upon the child's cognitive development, but is also influenced by its environment. For example, social learning theory proposes that children learn by **observing** models and **imitating** their behaviour. If this imitation is rewarded then the behaviour is more likely to persist. Albert Bandura used the term **self-efficacy** to refer to our belief that, through social learning processes, we can be effective in a particular type of situation (see p. 73). This is related to Cialdini's final stage, above, when the rewards for helping have become internalised.

The people who are likely to contribute to a child's socialisation are parents, siblings and peers as well as models provided in the media. Psychologists studying pro-social behaviour have found that:

- Parents who behave altruistically, as well as preaching altruism, had children who were more altruistic.

- Mothers who told children the consequences of their actions and who explained the rules clearly had children who were more likely to be helpful or sympathetic to others. (See Hoffman's research, p. 72.) Similarly, when older children were given reasons for being helpful, and encouraged to focus on how others feel, this increased their helping behaviour.

Nancy Eisenberg (1986) has noted that children from six years upwards show awareness that others may need help and she is one of several psychologists who have noted the link between helping others and developing friendships.

CRITICAL ANALYSIS OF FACTORS AFFECTING PRO-SOCIAL BEHAVIOUR

The social norms of equity and reciprocity include the notion of exchange, but **cross-cultural** research into helping behaviour shows that the emphasis on exchange is a Western trait which may be related to our more individualist cultures. In collectivist cultures there appears to be a universal norm to help, regardless of perceived need or closeness of relationship.

Whatever the social norms are, research in the West suggests that the degree to which we conform to social norms varies. There are many reasons for this, for example:

- some of these norms conflict so conforming to one means contravening another
- it depends how strongly we have internalised them
- it depends on the level and strength of our moral development
- it depends on our socialisation
- it depends on our judgements about other people; our interpretation of their motives and circumstances.

Social norms are therefore only a very general guide to who will help, why they will do so, who they will help and in what circumstances they will help. Similar criticisms arise when we look at socialisation, because there will be circumstances when the influence of parents will conflict, for example with the influence of peers, because different values apply in each case.

BYSTANDER INTERVENTION

In the first part of the chapter we considered reasons why people help others, but what encourages, or stops, people going to the assistance of those who need help? Research on this topic was triggered by the case of Kitty Genovese in New York, who was assaulted and stabbed to death outside her apartment one night. Despite her screams for help, she was attacked and sexually assaulted for more than half-an-hour, and finally she died. More than 30 people in the neighbouring apartments heard and saw the attack but did nothing to help until someone finally called the police. The term **bystander apathy** was used to describe this lack of action, and researchers started to examine what causes it.

THE DECISION MODEL OF BYSTANDER INTERVENTION

As a result of their research, Bibb Latané and John Darley (1970) proposed that apathy was a poor explanation for bystander inaction. They suggested that a bystander's decision to help goes through five stages, as shown in Figure 8.3 below.

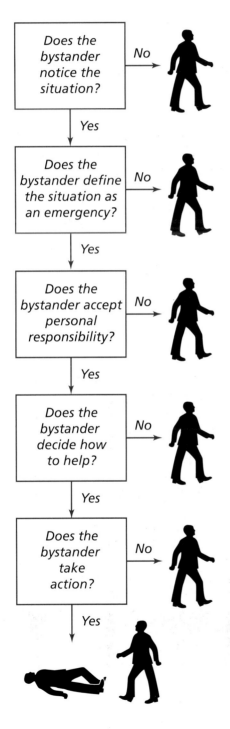

As we consider research related to these stages, you will note that we can identify several factors which affect bystander intervention.

DEFINING THE SITUATION

The bystander must first notice that something is happening and then decide whether it is an emergency. Is the person running towards you a shoplifter on the run or is he about to miss his bus? Are that man and woman who are arguing having a lovers' quarrel or is she about to be attacked? When we are uncertain we look to others for information (see Conformity, p. 30).

Latané and Darley (1968) tested the notion that we may fail to help because no-one else thinks help is needed. In their experiment, participants sat in a room completing a questionnaire. In one condition the participant was alone, in the other there were three participants.

Steam, which looked like smoke, started to pour into the room through an air vent: this continued for six minutes. The researchers observed the participants through a one-way window and noted how long it took them to report the smoke. The results are shown in Table 8.1.

Even though participants in a group failed to report the smoke, they were clearly bothered by it, wafting it from their eyes and coughing. Some said afterwards that they thought it might have been air-conditioning vapours or steam. Latané and Darley concluded that a situation which may be

Figure 8.3 *The five stages in the decision model of bystander intervention*

defined as an emergency by a single bystander can be defined as a non-emergency when there are several bystanders. This is known as **pluralistic ignorance**, and occurs when everyone misleads everyone else by defining the incident as a non-emergency.

Condition	Percentage of participants reporting smoke
Participant alone	75%
Participants with two others	13%

Table 8.1 *Results of Latané and Darley's (1968) smoke-filled room experiment*

Here we can see that one factor affecting bystander intervention is how other people behave. Others act as models, so here the bystander takes no action because others take none.

Critics argue that participants may have failed to go for help because they knew they were taking part in an experiment. Odd things happen in experiments, and participants try to work out what is really going on, so it may have been this, rather than awareness of others, which prohibited them from taking action.

In Chapter 3, under Conformity (p. 28), there is evidence that being part of a group influences our behaviour. The participant in the smoke-filled room was not simply a bystander, but was part of a group of three people all doing the same task together in a room. So group norms influenced the behaviour, but these would not necessarily be present in real-life emergencies.

ACCEPTING PERSONAL RESPONSIBILITY

Even when it has been defined as an emergency, does the bystander accept personal responsibility? Darley and Latané (1968) devised an experiment in which there was obviously an emergency – the participant heard someone having a seizure. Under what circumstances would the participant accept personal responsibility and take action?

Details of the research are described on p. 26 under Bystander Behaviour. The results showed that when participants thought they were the only ones to hear the seizure, 85 per cent of them quickly sought help. When they thought four others had heard the seizure only 35 per cent sought help, and waited longer before doing so.

Darley and Latané concluded that a factor affecting bystander intervention was how many people are present. The more 'others' that are present, the less likely any one person is to take personal responsibility for helping. They called this **diffusion of responsibility**. Later, when these participants were asked about their behaviour, many showed great concern about the seizure victim, particularly those who had taken least action.

Results from this research (and from the smoke-filled room study described earlier) suggest that another factor affecting bystander intervention is whether the bystander thinks he or she is the only one aware of the incident. In both studies the single bystander took action very quickly.

In subsequent research, when participants thought that the others were in a different building from the seizure victim, they were as likely to help as those who thought they were the only bystanders. This suggests that being close to the victim is another factor which makes us more likely to intervene.

Figure 8.4 *Could you explain this picture using some of the ideas from research into bystander intervention?*

Tom Moriarty (1975) conducted an experiment on a beach, where a confederate left some belongings on a towel. In the experimental condition he asked someone nearby to keep an eye on his belongings whilst he went away for a few minutes. In the control condition no-one was asked. In his absence a 'thief' stole his portable radio. The researchers found that 95 per cent of those who were asked to take responsibility gave chase, but in the control condition only 20 per cent of witnesses gave chase. However, the people who were asked to take responsibility could not be considered true 'bystanders'.

One factor which causes us to take personal responsibility is when we see someone similar to ourselves in need of help. This was investigated by C. Daniel Batson and his colleagues (1983) with participants who were divided into two groups. One group was told they were about to watch a woman who was similar to them, the other group thought the woman was not at all similar.

Each participant watched a woman (a confederate) on closed-circuit TV who was apparently receiving shocks in a learning experiment. As the shocks got worse, the woman told the researcher that due to a childhood experience she was very sensitive to shocks. The researcher then proposed that the participant, who was watching, might like to take her place. Results showed that participants who thought they were similar to the victim changed places more readily than those who thought they were dissimilar.

The results suggest that bystanders are more likely to intervene to help someone who is similar to them. Additional evidence comes from Piliavin's (1969) subway studies, which are described below. Batson's explanation for this is that we have greater empathy for those we see as being similar to ourselves. This creates arousal when we see them in distress, and we intervene in order to reduce our arousal.

KNOWING HOW TO HELP

Even when the bystander accepts personal responsibility, the decision to intervene may depend on their ability to help. For example, a young woman who sees a youngster being attacked by several others may not know how to stop them. A study which arranged for students and nurses to witness an accident showed that the nurses were more likely to help and the students held back. However, when there was not a nurse present, students helped as readily as the nurses had before. These results support Latané and Darley's proposal that bystanders make a series of decisions before they intervene.

TAKING ACTION

There are a number of factors which affect the likelihood that bystanders who have reached this stage in the decision-making process will take action. Some of these are suggested in the research by Irving Piliavin and his colleagues (1969). They devised a series of studies to investigate the effects that the type of victim, the race of the victim and the presence of a model have on helping behaviour. The procedure was that two confederates played a 'victim' who collapsed and a helper who came to his aid. This was acted out in a carriage of the New York subway system.

SAMPLING

The researchers used opportunity sampling in their 'subway' studies; participants were people who were sitting in the area where the victim collapsed. They were people who were travelling on the New York subway between 11 a.m. and 3 p.m. when the trials were conducted. There was a mean of 8.5 participants in the 103 trials. The sample comprised approximately 45 per cent black and 55 per cent white male and female participants.

The **conditions** were varied – sometimes the victim was white, sometimes black, sometimes carrying a cane, sometimes appearing to be drunk and sometimes apparently bleeding from the mouth. Sometimes the 'helper' model waited one minute before helping, other times he waited two and a half minutes. Both victim and helper were male. Two **observers** noted information such as the characteristics of the participants who helped, how long it took and what comments were made.

The results showed that:

- the 'cane' victim was helped immediately in almost every trial and regardless of his race
- the victim who appeared to be drunk or bleeding was helped 50 per cent of the time before the 'helper' model intervened
- the drunk victim was more likely to be helped by someone of the same race
- several people helped
- as soon as one person made a move to help, several others followed
- men were much more likely to help than women
- the number of other bystanders had little effect on the rate of helping.

The researchers concluded that people do help in an emergency to a greater degree than laboratory experiments would suggest. Even though there were many bystanders there was no evidence of less helping (diffusion of responsibility) and there seemed little evidence of pluralistic ignorance because people acted quickly.

However this research does support some of the laboratory experiments, insofar as there was more helping when it was easier to know what to do. There was more helping of the 'cane' victim than the 'drunk', whose condition and possible reaction were unknown. This difference could also be explained by the social norm of equity (see p. 85).

In addition, there was no ambiguity about the situation and participants were close by. Proximity to the victim, as a factor affecting bystander intervention, was also evident in the 'seizure' research by Darley and Latané.

The results of the subway studies add to the evidence that a factor affecting bystander behaviour is whether someone provides a model for helping. This was also found in the research of J. Bryan and M. Test (1967) when more people stopped to help a woman with a flat tyre if they had just seen a man helping a different woman with a flat tyre (see p. 27 for details).

One of the criticisms of Piliavin's research is that many **ethical guidelines** were contravened. For example, participants did not consent to participate; they were deceived; witnesses of the 'emergency' may have experienced distress and it was not possible to debrief them afterwards. Some of these problems are common in field experiments, which take place in a real-life setting. There are also problems of experimental control.

EXPERIMENTAL CONTROL

The study by Piliavin and his colleagues (1969) is an example of a field experiment. Psychologists value field experiments because whatever is being studied occurs in a natural setting so participants will not be affected by the artificiality of a laboratory setting. If the participants are unaware that they are taking part in an experiment, their behaviour will not be affected by demand characteristics. However, researchers are unable to exert as much control as they could in a laboratory setting.

For example, in the 'subway' research:

- Most of the participants may have been from the same socioeconomic class or of similar ages; because the experimenter cannot select the participants they are unlikely to be a representative sample of the population.
- The observers may have been unable to note everything which everbody did because there was simply too much happening at one time or because their view was obscured.

FACTORS AFFECTING BYSTANDER INTERVENTION

When they started their work on bystander behaviour, Latané and Darley used the term 'bystander apathy' for the lack of response which bystanders showed in real-life emergencies. The research evidence described above suggests that it is not apathy which explains why people fail to help, but a number of other factors such as:

- when the bystander knows he is the only one aware of the emergency
- when the bystander knows how to help
- similarity to the victim
- the number of other bystanders
- the behaviour of other bystanders – as a model of either helping behaviour or inaction
- how close the bystander is to the victim.

Whilst these factors affect bystander behaviour, several of them may be present in a situation. They may have an additive effect (the victim is similar and someone else has gone to help), making it more likely the bystander will help. But they may also have a contradictory effect (the victim is similar but no-one else has taken any action). This creates conflict for the bystander which may in turn delay their response. We have also seen that even when bystanders have failed to act, they nevertheless experience anxiety and some distress about the well-being of the victim. However, the factors we have considered may be so powerful that they still inhibit action, despite this anxiety.

Sample Exam Questions

1 What do psychologists mean by the term 'altruism'?
   (2 marks)

2 With reference to the work of Hoffman, explain two stages in the development of empathy.
   (4 marks)

3 a Identify one social norm. *(1 mark)*
   b Explain how it may affect pro-social behaviour. *(3 marks)*

4 Identify two factors affecting bystander intervention.
   (2 marks)

5 Discuss two ways in which other people might affect bystander intervention.
   (3 + 3 marks)

6 Describe and evaluate one study in which bystander intervention was investigated.
   (8 marks)

Anti-social Behaviour

People may say others are aggressive when referring to their manner of speaking, their body language, the way they play a sport or the way they treat others. Our concern here is the kind of aggression which is intentional and destructive. What causes this behaviour? What role do parents play? How can aggression be reduced? This chapter looks at psychology's attempts to answer these questions.

EXPLANATIONS FOR AGGRESSION

Aggression is regarded as **anti-social behaviour** and is generally considered to be behaviour which harms, or intends to harm, someone or something. Aggression can be verbal as well as physical. We will begin by considering a variety of explanations which, as you will see, reflect different ways of explaining human behaviour. Then we look at the way that parents might influence their child's aggression and finally we review some possible ways of reducing aggression.

ETHOLOGICAL APPROACH

Ethology is the study of animals in their natural environment and ethologists are interested in how animal behaviours increase their chances of survival and of repro-duction. The ethologist Konrad Lorenz (1966) called aggression the 'fighting instinct'. It is used by animals for survival, to gain food, to gain a mate, and to protect their territory from others of the same species.

All instincts generate a drive or energy which is constantly renewed and which therefore must be released. If aggressive energy remains unused, the excess may be used destructively on other members of the species. Lorenz proposed that animals had evolved ways of releasing excess energy which are not destructive. These are known as rituals. For example:

- **Threat gestures** enable an animal to warn another that it is prepared to fight. The hair or feathers may become erect, some animals bare their teeth and those with horns lower their heads. Two animals may do this until one of them withdraws. If this does not happen then **ritualised fighting** occurs.
- **Ritualised fighting** is fighting which shows a stereotypical pattern for each species, and stops before serious injury occurs. Male antelopes lock and push their horns

but rarely gore each other. The first animal to 'give in' will show this by the use of **appeasement gestures**.

- **Appeasement gestures** enable an animal who is fighting to indicate submission to the other. The gesture is one that shows the animal's vulnerability, so when two cats are fighting the 'loser' turns away from the 'winner' and shows its neck. The 'loser' is showing its vulnerability since the 'winner' could now inflict real injury, but in fact it stops. Lorenz said this particular behaviour is ritualised in cats and inhibits the aggression of the 'winner'.

Because animals of the same species show the same behaviours that are specific to that species, Lorenz claimed that they are innate: they have evolved through many generations. What has this got to do with human aggression? Lorenz claimed that aggression fulfilled similar purposes for humans. We are, by nature, warriors, likely to solve conflicts using aggression. We also have **threat** and **appeasement** gestures, such as smiling, kneeling or bowing the head. However, with the development of weapons of destruction (bombs, guns, etc.) which separate human aggressors from each other, these appeasement gestures cannot come into effect. Human aggression is therefore potentially deadly, because smiling or bowing cannot be seen by someone who is, for example, dropping a bomb.

Figure 9.1 *Weapons which separate aggressors prevent our instinctive appeasement gestures from overriding our aggression, according to Lorenz*

More recent ethological research has shown that animals such as chimpanzees do kill members of their own species, sometimes even the infants. This weakens Lorenz's argument. But humans are much more complex than non-humans, and we should not **generalise** directly from non-human to human behaviour. This complexity is evident in our many different cultures, and cross-cultural research shows wide variations in the levels of aggression in different societies, suggesting social factors are more influential than innate factors.

BIOLOGICAL APPROACH

From a biological perspective, researchers have looked at the role of the brain, hormones and chemicals in aggression. The **limbic system**, which is a primitive part of the **central nervous system**, is linked to aggression. For example, in some animals damage to the limbic system increases aggression and decreases fear. However, damage to the **amygdala**, which is part of the limbic system, results in timidity. Research on human brains has been restricted to people with very severe problems requiring brain surgery, although more recent developments in brain scanning have considerably extended the possibilities for research.

The case of Charles Whitman provides an example of how brain damage may cause aggression. Charles Whitman shot his mother, his wife and then more than a dozen students at the University of Texas in1966 before being killed by police. Prior to this he had sought help for the overwhelming violent impulses he was experiencing and asked that an autopsy be performed on him after his death to see if there was any physical disorder. The autopsy revealed a tumour in or very near his amygdala.

Psychosurgery to the amygdala has been reported as successfully reducing violent behaviour in other patients, but it may affect other functions as well. Damage to the amygdala may also affect a person's ability to read emotional cues (such as facial expressions or tone of voice) or to understand dangerous situations.

The biological approach also indicates that higher levels of certain chemicals or hormones are linked to aggression. For example, the higher levels of aggression generally shown by males are associated with their higher levels of **testosterone**. Research has shown that violent criminals show higher levels of testosterone than non-violent criminals. But higher levels of this hormone have also been found in dominant, but non-violent, criminals. This suggests that the relationship between aggression and testosterone is complex.

Serotonin has also been linked to aggression and this could be associated with its influence on the **reticular activating system**. This RAS keeps us alert to sensory information but serotonin dampens down this effect. Research suggests that lower levels of serotonin are related to higher levels of aggression, perhaps allowing the RAS to be too responsive.

This very brief survey indicates how complex the study of human aggression is from the biological perspective. Critics also argue that this view fails to take account of cognition and socialisation in the expression, or inhibition, of human aggression.

PSYCHODYNAMIC APPROACH

The main tenet of this approach is that aggression is innate, and there are two explanations based on this view.

SIGMUND FREUD'S THEORY
Freud proposed that each of us has an instinct for self-destruction (the death instinct or **thanatos**) and that aggression is the drive which enables us to satisfy this instinct. Like Lorenz, Freud argued that aggressive urges are constantly building up within us, and have to be released in order to prevent a sudden explosion of aggression.

Our death instinct conflicts with our life instinct (called the **libido**), yet both these instincts are constantly in need of satisfaction. Freud proposed that the **ego** (the part of our personality which tries to satisfy our instincts in a realistic way) manages these conflicting instincts and avoids self-destruction by directing our self-destructive energy outwards. We need to do this in a way which meets the demands of our **superego** (see p. 77), which is the moral part of personality, so we use:

- **sublimation** – channelling aggression into acceptable activities, such as sport
- **displacement** – transferring aggression outwards onto someone, or something, else.

Other psychodynamic theorists assert that aggression can be controlled without damage if the ego and superego are strong enough. Some of the elements of Freud's explanation were subsequently linked to learning theory to produce the frustration–aggression hypothesis.

THE FRUSTRATION–AGGRESSION HYPOTHESIS

J. Dollard and his associates (1939) combined Freud's belief that aggression is innate with learning theory. They proposed that aggression is caused by frustration, and therefore that anyone who is frustrated will be aggressive. This became known as the **frustration–aggression hypothesis**, which proposes that people are motivated to reach goals, but if they are blocked, then frustration occurs. For example, if a task is too difficult or someone stops us from doing something, we will become frustrated. When we are frustrated, we aggress.

Like Freud, this explanation argues that aggression may be delayed or directed onto a target other than the cause of the frustration. An example of this is **scapegoating**, when aggression is turned onto an individual or group who is not the cause of frustration but who is a 'safe' target because they are less powerful and not likely to retaliate (see Prejudice, p. 18).

However, some studies have shown that aggression is only raised slightly when participants are frustrated. N. Miller (1941) identified several reasons why an individual might not show aggressive behaviour. They might:

- think it wrong to behave aggressively
- have learned not to show aggression
- be frightened that the other person would be aggressive towards them
- think that although the other person made them frustrated, it was not done intentionally.

Accordingly, the hypothesis was modified to state that frustration may cause aggression.

So aggression is not always shown; whether it is or not depends on the individual's past experiences, the other people involved in the situation and its meaning for the individual. In addition, frustration may lead to other consequences, such as apathy or hopelessness.

The notion of frustration has been taken up by Leonard Berkowitz (1968) who argued that frustration does not cause aggression directly but does arouse anger. The anger in turn creates a readiness to act aggressively. If there are aggressive cues in the environment – a gun, for example – this makes the individual more likely to be aggressive. He demonstrated this in a series of experiments in which participants were angered by someone. This person was a confederate in the experiment.

Participants were then given the opportunity to deliver mild shocks to him. Some participants saw a shotgun and revolver next to the shock switches, and some of these participants were told they belonged to the person who had made them angry. Another group saw neutral objects such as a badminton racket and a **control group** saw no other objects.

The results showed that more shocks were delivered by participants who saw the guns than those in the groups that saw a badminton racket or no objects. Berkowitz proposed that people learn to associate particular stimuli (such as a gun, or a boxing match, or a person) with anger or ways of releasing anger. When the individual is frustrated this creates anger and a gun, for example, becomes a cue for aggression. This explanation for aggression is linked to the principles of learning theory, and like social learning theory it stresses the role of situational cues in determining whether aggression occurs.

SOCIAL LEARNING APPROACH

This explanation proposes that aggression comes from **observing** the aggression of others and **imitating** it. **Reinforcement** and **punishment** also play a part in social learning theory (see Chapter 11, pp. 123–125 for details of these terms). The main principles were devised by Albert Bandura and his colleagues as a result of many studies of aggression.

In Bandura's early experiments, an adult modelled aggressive behaviour towards a large inflatable doll – called a Bobo doll. The adult hit it with a mallet (physical aggression) and spoke aggressively ('Hit him', 'Kick him'). Children of three to five years old watched this and then had the opportunity to play with the doll. The photographs in Figure 9.2 were taken during these experiments.

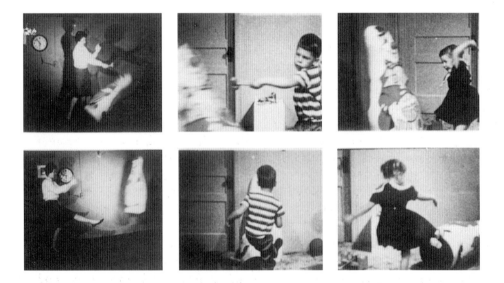

Figure 9.2 *Here you can see the aggressive behaviour of a female model, and the subsequent behaviour of a boy and girl who watched the model (from A. Bandura et al., 1961)*

The children showed significantly more imitation of a same-sex model and boys performed more acts of aggression than girls, as Table 9.1 shows.

Participant's gender	Female model	Male model
Female	19	9
Male	17	38

Table 9.1 *Mean scores of imitative aggression of a male and a female model (from A. Bandura et al., 1961)*

In variations on this procedure, Bandura and his colleagues divided the participants into three groups, each seeing a different consequence after the model's aggression. The observations showed that seeing a model punished resulted in the lowest levels of imitative behaviour, as you can see in Table 9.2.

Consequences for model	Children's level of imitative aggression
Model punished after being aggressive	lowest level
No consequences after being aggressive	higher level
Model reinforced after being aggressive	highest level

Table 9.2 *Bandura's three conditions and participants' level of aggression*

Bandura and his colleagues concluded that children exposed to aggressive models may imitate the aggressive behaviour and are more likely to do so if the model is the same sex or if their aggression is reinforced (which is called **vicarious reinforcement**). Children are less likely to imitate aggression if the model is punished. This research also provided evidence that children knew what behaviour was appropriate for the models, because some of them commented that 'ladies shouldn't do things like that'.

When the children were asked to reproduce as much of the model's behaviour as they could remember, (and were rewarded for doing this), all of them were able to reproduce most of the aggressive acts. This was true even with children who had seen the model punished (which had resulted in the lowest level of imitation). We can conclude that all the children had learned the behaviour, but the likelihood of them imitating it depended on factors such as the sex of the model and whether the model's performance of the behaviour was rewarded or punished.

Reinforcement is an important explanation for why children might persist in these imitative acts. This is what Gerald Patterson and his colleagues (1967) found in their observational study of young children. They noted acts of interpersonal aggression and the immediate consequences of the actions. Results showed that for children showing the highest levels of aggression, the most common consequence was a rewarding one for the child. Children who were aggressive and then punished (the victim fought back) were the least likely to be aggressive.

However, Patterson found evidence of **negative reinforcement** in children who were not very aggressive. If they sometimes fought back when they were attacked, they gradually became more aggressive themselves. Overall, these results suggest that if aggressive behaviour is reinforced it is more likely to be repeated.

Reinforcement also explains why aggressive behaviour might take place in one situation but not in another. For example, a child might learn that his teacher disapproves when he acts out a violent scene from a film he has watched, so he no longer performs it in front of the teacher. But this behaviour wins admiration from his peers, so he does it in the playground, out of the teacher's sight.

Critics of the social learning approach assert that it overemphasises the influence of the environment and experience and underestimates the importance of inherited or biological factors. Although it does incorporate aspects of cognition, it does not put enough emphasis on the human ability to reason or consider moral issues.

SUMMARY OF EXPLANATIONS FOR AGGRESSION

Critics of laboratory experiments of aggression question whether results can be **generalised** to everyday life. Examples are the studies by Berkowitz and by Bandura. More naturalistic methods, such as Patterson's observations of children, show the complexity of human aggression.

To summarise, the ethological and psychodynamic approaches view aggression as innate, and the biological approach focuses on innate and physical causes. Social learning theorists propose that aggression is learned from others in our society, through exposure to aggressive behaviour and the way it is reinforced when it is performed. Table 9.3 summarises some distinctions between these four explanations of aggression.

	Ethological	Biological	Psychodynamic	Social learning
Origins	innate drive to ensure survival	innate and/or physical	innate drive – thanatos or frustration	learned from observing others and reinforcement
Implications	must be released	biological treatment	must be released	society responsible
Controlled by	innate ritualised behaviours	chemicals or surgery	ego and superego cognitive or environmental factors	punishment, non-aggressive models

Table 9.3 *Summary of some distinctions between different explanations of aggression*

WAYS OF REDUCING AGGRESSION

Of course, one of the reasons for studying aggression is to identify ways in which it can be reduced. Below are descriptions of methods which are based on the explanations we have considered above.

ETHOLOGICAL APPROACH

The ethological approach argues that aggression must be discharged, and that this can be achieved without serious harm by the use of **ritualised** behaviours. People who work in situations where aggression is likely (such as policing, the prison service or psychiatric units) can be trained to avoid using **threat gestures** and to use **appeasement gestures** in order to stop a confrontation from escalating. For example, when facing a potentially aggressive person do not stand face-to-face, speak calmly and softly and use slow, relaxed movements.

Figure 9.3 *This police officer's stance is relaxed. He is using an appeasement gesture to stop the confrontation from escalating*

This approach would also suggest the removal of guns and other weapons since they prevent appeasement gestures from operating. However, there can still be high levels of aggression and violence when there are no weapons involved, and when people use appeasement gestures to try to de-escalate a situation. This suggests this explanation of aggression has limitations.

One of the possible outlets for aggression in a ritualised setting is sport. Indeed the type of behaviour which is acceptable in a sport setting but not in everyday life has been called **channelled aggression,** if it is not accompanied by anger. Examples would be tackling in rugby or punching in boxing. So sport can provide a 'safe' outlet for aggression, according to ethological theory.

This is not always the case, of course, because the rules are created by humans; they are not a result of evolution. The competitive and confrontational nature of the sport setting, combined with physical contact, seems to increase aggression rather than provide an opportunity to simply discharge it. Evidence for this comes from research such as that by Arms and his colleagues (1979) which is described on page 103.

BIOLOGICAL APPROACH

The biological approach would suggest that aggression could be reduced through the use of surgery or chemicals in the form of drugs. As we have seen, surgery on the amygdala has reduced aggression in very violent people, although this is a complex and extreme form of treatment with deep ethical implications. This is also true of castration, even though it has been found to reduce aggression in very violent men.

The causes and nature of aggression are very complex and interconnected. Because we do not fully understand which parts of the brain and what processes are involved in aggression, it is difficult to devise treatments for specific problems. So aggression may be reduced by drugs which slow down or lower the body's response to stimuli, but these drugs may also cause drowsiness, inability to concentrate, loss of memory, loss of appetite and so on. This in turn may lead to the person losing their job, poor health or deterioration in social relationships, which may be more damaging than the original condition.

PSYCHODYNAMIC APPROACH

This approach is similar to the ethological approach in that both see aggression as constantly building up. Sport provides an opportunity for **sublimation** – channelling aggression into acceptable activities. But Freud also argued that simply watching competitive sport was cathartic; it released pent-up aggression.

Figure 9.4 *Watching or taking part in sport should reduce aggression according to Freud*

However, some research contradicts this claim. R. Arms and colleagues (1979) compared the effects of watching high-contact sports (wrestling and ice hockey) with a swimming event. Participants watching wrestling and ice hockey experienced increased feelings of hostility, whereas those watching swimming did not. These results suggest that watching competitive sport is not cathartic; indeed it may lead to increased aggression for spectators of high-contact sports.

Freud also argued that the **displacement** of aggression prevents us from destroying ourselves. This involves transferring aggression outwards and onto someone, or something, else. To avoid aggressing against others, this aggression should be directed at objects. Punching a cushion, throwing a soft ball at the wall or digging vigorously in the garden should all release aggression.

This may be effective with objects, but research in a laboratory setting suggests the opposite effect when aggression is directed towards people. When participants are given the chance to shock another person who cannot retaliate, participants became more punitive, giving higher levels of shock. Leonard Berkowitz (1965) found that participants who were angry became even more punitive, whereas Freud would predict that they would become less punitive as their aggression was released.

The amended frustration–aggression hypothesis suggests that if people are encouraged to interpret frustration in a different way, such as finding a positive aspect of it ('the TV is broken, oh well I can get some homework done') or learn ways of controlling their own tendency to aggress ('take a deep breath and relax') this may prevent frustration leading to aggression. This may be more effective at reducing aggression than watching or taking part in aggressive activities.

SOCIAL LEARNING APPROACH

According to social learning theory, if we see models who are punished for aggression, we should be less likely to show aggression. This is what Bandura found, as we saw earlier in Table 9.2, but seeing non-aggressive models can also reduce aggression, according to research by Robert Baron (1977). He gave participants the opportunity to give electric shocks to someone. In fact this person was a confederate who pretended to be receiving the shocks. The experimental group of participants had previously seen a non-aggressive model and the control group had not seen a model. Baron found that those seeing a non-aggressive model gave fewer shocks than those seeing no model, which suggests that seeing non-aggressive models can reduce aggression.

Aggressive models, however, cannot be totally removed from society. The media has frequently been blamed for providing models for aggressive behaviour, but it also provides non-aggressive models. J. Murray (1980) investigated the behaviour of children after watching some of the programmes on American TV which promoted helpfulness and sharing. Results showed that the children's helpful and sharing behaviour increased.

RESEARCH INTO CHILD-REARING STYLES AND AGGRESSIVE BEHAVIOUR

As we might expect from the material we have already covered in this chapter, there is considerable evidence that the way parents bring up their children is related to the levels of aggression the children show. Let us look first at two studies which produced very similar results.

Diana Baumrind (1967) observed families with pre-school children, noting several aspects of the parents' behaviour towards their children, namely:

- the amount of warmth the parents showed
- how clear and consistent the parents' rules were
- how independent children were expected to be
- how much the parents talked to and listened to their children.

A study by Robert Sears (1977) and his colleagues looked at how 379 parents in Boston disciplined their five-year-old children. Six years later they followed up the children to assess their levels of aggression and moral development. From the results of both of these studies, the researchers concluded that there were three distinctive **child-rearing styles**:

- **Permissive** parents were warm but were inconsistent with rules. They made few demands on their children, they did not discuss or explain things and used little discipline. Their children tended to be aggressive and remain aggressive.
- **Authoritarian** parents were not warm, nor did they discuss or explain things. They set many rules, expected obedience and disciplined their children often and quite harshly. Their children were aggressive when young, though they were less aggressive but more anxious six years later.
- **Democratic** (or **authoritative**) parents were warm, explained to their children what was expected of them and why, and made rules clear and consistent: discipline was restrained and fair. They were flexible and encouraged their children in family decision-making. Their children were less aggressive and remained that way.

Eleanor Maccoby and John Martin (1983) have added a fourth child-rearing style:

- **Neglecting** or **rejecting** parents rejected or were indifferent to their children and therefore did not get involved in child-rearing. These children tended to show higher levels of aggression, and difficulties in their relationships with others, which persisted as they grew up. This could be linked to attachments, which is discussed in Chapter 4.

The research by Sears revealed that parents permitted their sons to be more aggressive than their daughters. It also showed that mothers who used psychological punishment (withdrawal of love) for bad behaviour tended to have children with a more highly developed conscience than children who were deprived of privileges or given physical punishment after bad behaviour. In addition, punishment was more effective if given by someone who had a warm relationship with the child.

Leonard Eron (1982) provides research evidence which illustrates how the democratic parenting style may reduce aggression. He studied the parents' role in helping children understand the aggression they have seen in the media. When adults talk

Figure 9.5 *The way a parent handles punishment can affect a child's level of aggression*

about the consequences of the violence their children watch, or have children discuss and write about the harmful effects, these children show lower levels of aggression in the following weeks. This suggests that cognitive factors which increase understanding of aggressive behaviour can reduce aggression.

CRITICAL EVALUATION

Research such as the studies described above depends to a considerable extent on the parents' reports of both their own, and their child's, behaviour. They may have given answers which reflected what was socially desirable (see below) rather than accurate. Indeed, the issue of accuracy is a complex one in this type of research, because our behaviour varies considerably from day to day and from situation to situation. A parent may discipline strictly if their child lies yet be permissive about being rude.

SOCIAL DESIRABILITY IN INTERVIEWS
In an interview the researcher asks the questions face-to-face but this may encourage people to give socially desirable answers. Parents in the Baumrind (1967) and Sears (1977) research may have been reluctant to say how often or harshly they disciplined, being aware that society disapproves of cruelty to children. Indeed, the parents who said they discussed moral behaviour and reasons for punishment with their children also gave more restrained and appropriate punishment. These parents may have been more aware of society's standards of upbringing and of appropriate discipline, whereas the parent with the authoritarian style may have been less concerned about what other people think – ignoring both their children's and society's views.

Another difficulty in this research is that when children are reared by two parents, each of whom may have a different style, it is not possible to determine which style is related to which aspects of the child's behaviour.

Finally, of course, much of the evidence we have looked at here is correlational, so we cannot conclude that parents cause particular behaviours in their children. There are many variables which can affect both the child-rearing style of the parents and the child's behaviour. For instance, family circumstances such as poverty, poor health or lack of social support may influence the behaviour of both parent and child.

Sample Exam Questions

1 Describe how the biological approach explains aggression.
   (3 marks)

2 Describe two ways in which the ethological approach differs from the social learning approach as an explanation for aggression.
   (4 marks)

3 Describe one study in which the reduction of aggression has been investigated. Indicate in your answer the method used, the results obtained and the conclusions drawn.
   (4 marks)

4 Describe the democratic style of child-rearing.
   (3 marks)

5 Discuss one difficulty in studying the way parents rear their children.
   (3 marks)

6 Using your knowledge of psychology, discuss how parents might influence their children's behaviour.
   (8 marks)

Perception

It could be argued that vision is the most important of our senses, as the vast majority of the information about the external world reaches us through our eyes. Corresponding with this, a larger part of the brain is involved in vision than any other sense. As you look at this page light waves enter your eye, but it is your visual perception which enables you to organise them into a pattern of black and white marks which you understand as letter shapes. Psychologists have investigated how we interpret these patterns, what role our visual system plays and what part experience plays. We will look at some of these ideas in this chapter, and consider why our perception is sometimes wrong.

THE VISUAL SYSTEM

When you look at this page the marks are picked up by your eyes in the form of light energy. This light energy is changed into electrical impulses which then travel to the brain where they are interpreted. How does this occur? The processing of this information starts with light entering the eye and passing through the cornea, the pupil and the lens, and it then strikes the retina. An illustration of this is shown in Figure 10.1, and the function of each part of the eye is described below.

- The **cornea** focuses or bends light and protects the eye.
- The **pupil** is the hole in the **iris** through which light waves pass. Its size is adjusted by the iris so that in bright light the pupil becomes smaller and in dim light it enlarges to allow more light to enter.
- The **lens** focuses the light onto the area of visual acuity.
- The **retina** converts light energy into electrical impulses via photo receptors which are called either rods or cones.
- The **optic nerve** transmits the electrical impulses to the visual cortex in the brain for decoding.

These electrical impulses are transmitted down the optic nerve of each eye to the **optic chiasma**. Information picked up in the left visual field goes to the right side of each eye (and vice versa), as you can see in the diagram showing the **visual pathways** (Figure 10.2). The nerve fibres that pass close to the nose cross over to the other hemisphere when they reach the optic chiasma, whilst those from the outer part of the eye continue in the same hemisphere.

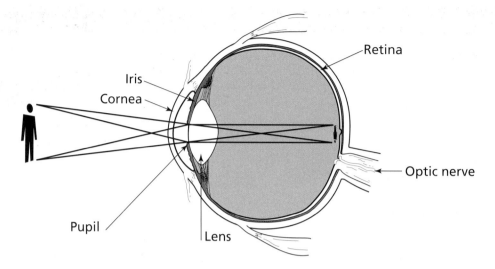

Figure 10.1 *Diagram of the human eye*

From the optic chiasma information goes on to the **visual cortex**. As you can see from Figure 10.2, information from the right visual field is processed in the left hemisphere, and information from the left field is processed in the right hemisphere.

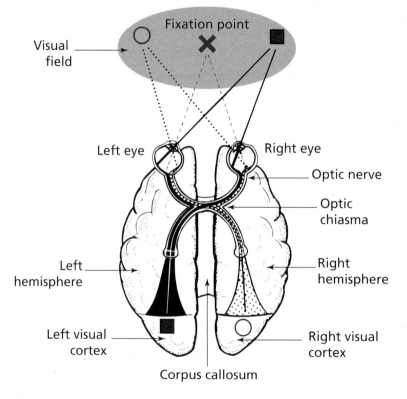

Figure 10.2 *The visual pathways*

SENSATION AND PERCEPTION

Sensation refers to the physical stimulation of the sensory receptors. In Figure 10.1 you can see that the image which strikes the retina is upside down and two dimensional, so how is it that we perceive it the right way up and three dimensionally? This is **perception** – the process of interpreting and understanding sensory information. An illustration of the difference between sensation and perception is the image in Figure 10.3a. We see it as a cube, then it appears to change to a cube seen from a different angle. We perceive two different cubes, yet the sensory information (the image on the retina) has not changed.

VISUAL ILLUSIONS

In visual illusions our perception interprets visual information so that we 'see' something different from what is actually there. Four examples of how we misinterpret visual information are shown in Figure 10.3.

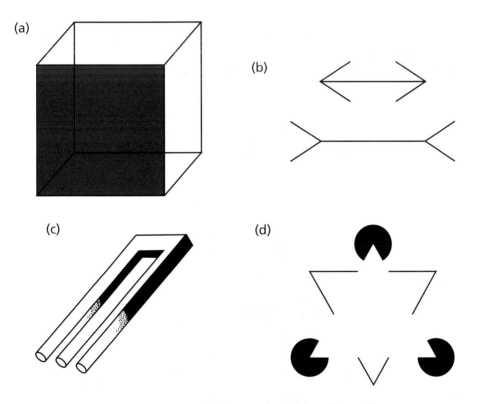

(a)

(b)

(c)

(d)

Figure 10.3 *Visual illusions – (a) the Necker cube, (b) Müller–Lyer, (c) devil's pitchfork and (d) Kanizska triangle*

- **Ambiguity** (Figure 10.3a) – if you look at the red face of the Necker cube it appears to jump and the configuration of the cube changes. This is called **depth reversal**. We cannot see both configurations at the same time, and we seem unable to control when the change occurs.

- **Distortion** (Figure 10.3b) – in the Müller–Lyer illusion both these lines are of equal length, yet we perceive the line with the outgoing fins as longer.
- **Paradox** (Figure 10.3c) – we see what is sometimes called the 'devil's pitchfork', yet an object like this cannot exist. How many prongs does it have?
- **Fiction** (Figure 10.3d) – we see a figure when there is no outline to define it. In the Kanizska triangle not only do we see a triangle where none is defined, but it appears to be a brighter white than its background.

EVERYDAY EXAMPLES OF VISUAL ILLUSIONS

One of the most common illusions occurs when we watch films. The images on films appear to move exactly as we see them in real life, but films are comprised of a series of still pictures presented very rapidly. They convey the effect of continuous movement because each still image is briefly retained on the retina so that the sequence of slightly different images appears continuous.

Another fiction, called the **phi phenomenon,** is used in electronic noticeboards. When a sequence of lights goes on and off very rapidly one after the other, it appears as if the light is moving. This is how notices are displayed on public information systems.

PERCEPTION AS A MODELLING PROCESS

Some psychologists have seen perception as driven by our expectations, which provide models of what to expect. An example of this approach is described below.

GREGORY'S EXPLANATIONS OF VISUAL ILLUSIONS

Richard Gregory (1977) proposed that an enormous amount of information reaches the eye, but much is lost by the time it reaches the brain. There could be more than one interpretation of the information, so the brain has to do some guessing. It does this based on past experience, which provides models for future use – hypotheses. We interpret the sensory information in terms of these models, but as a result we often misinterpret the information and may make mistakes, thus creating visual illusions.

Gregory suggests that the brain forms hypotheses about what is being seen, tests them and chooses the one which seems most correct. This causes difficulties in the perception of the Necker cube in Figure 10.3 because there are two equally likely interpretations. Gregory proposes that we test each of them and they both seem correct, so our perception alternates between them. However, the other illusions are not ambiguous.

In the Müller–Lyer illusion we are using our knowledge of perspective to interpret the two images. Figure 10.4 illustrates this, showing the outgoing fins as the far corner of a room and the ingoing fins as the near corner of a building. Gregory claims that, based on our previous experience of perspective, we 'scale up' the far corner to compensate for it being further away (for more on scaling up see Perception of Size on p. 114).

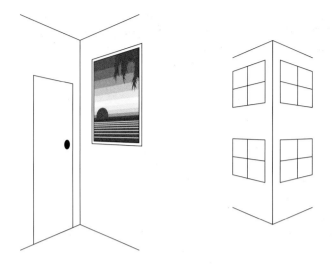

Figure 10.4 *An intepretation of the Müller–Lyer illusion*

However, this explanation is undermined when we look at the images in Figure 10.5 in which the 'fins' (which are the **perspective cues**) have been removed. The illusion that one line is longer than the other still remains.

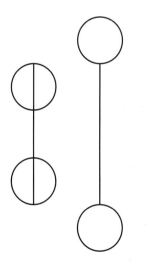

Figure 10.5 *The Müller–Lyer illusion with perspective cues removed*

Gregory's explanation for the paradoxical figure (Figure 10.3c) is that we have to see it as more than lines on a page – using past experience we create a hypothesis for what it is. We then test this hypothesis, we see the object we have 'imposed' on the pattern of lines and realise it cannot exist. Each side of the image 'makes sense' yet we are unable to integrate them so that the whole image makes sense.

In his explanation for the Kanizska triangle in Figure 10.3d, Gregory proposes that we infer contours, based on previous experience that an object will mask another object when it is placed in front of it (see Overlap, p. 113). We hypothesise that a triangle is masking the three black circles but the triangle itself is a fiction.

PERCEPTION OF DISTANCE

Distance perception refers to the ways in which we perceive how far away objects are. This is also referred to as **depth perception,** because objects appear at various depths in the visual field. The image that falls on the retina is two dimensional, so how can we perceive depth? We can do this using information from both eyes (binocular cues) or one eye (monocular cues).

BINOCULAR DEPTH CUES

- **Retinal disparity** – because each eye looks at the world from a slightly different point, we get two slightly different views of an object. Try this yourself by holding a pencil at arm's length, closing one eye and lining the pencil up against the window or a corner of the room. Now close this eye and open the other: the pencil 'jumps' to one side. This is because you are seeing it from a different point – from your other eye. With both eyes open, the brain is receiving these two different sets of information which create retinal disparity. The amount of retinal disparity which the brain registers gives an indication of the distance away of the object.
- **Ocular convergence** – the nearer an object is, the more the eyes turn inwards (converge) in order to see the object. Information passes from the eye muscles to the brain. It tells the brain how much the eyes have turned and so helps us to perceive how close, or far away, an object is.

These binocular depth cues provide direct information for the interpretation of visual information.

MONOCULAR DEPTH CUES

We can still perceive depth using only one eye because of visual cues in our environment. Some examples are shown in Figure 10.6.

These cues are used to show depth (three dimensions) in pictures (which are two dimensional). However, James Gibson (1966) argues that in the real world there is much information available directly; an example is given in binocular cues above. Gibson considers that perception is direct, not subject to hypothesis testing as Gregory proposed. Objects are perceived within their environment and we know this environment from past experience. In addition, movement is part of our perception, which is a factor Gregory took insufficient account of.

Rather than study perception from the point of view of an image on the retina, Gibson stressed that the eyes receive a constant stream of light, and as we move around the patterns of light change, which he calls the **optic array**. Gibson says we judge distance using, for example, **texture gradient**. This is illustrated in Figure 10. 7 and refers to the way in which closer objects are larger and clearer than those further away. On a pebbly beach the closest pebbles are the largest, but as you walk along it is not the pebbles themselves which indicate depth but the way their size changes as you move.

Another example supporting Gibson's argument that perception is direct is **motion parallax**, which is evident when sitting on a fast-moving train. As we move through our environment, objects which are close to us pass by faster than those further away. The relative speed of these objects indicates their distance away from us.

 **Overlap** – if one object hides part of another, the complete object is closer

 **Height in the visual field** – the closer to the horizon that the object is, the further away it is

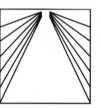 **Relative size** – larger objects are closer

Linear perspective – parallel lines converge as they recede into the distance

Figure 10.6 *Some monocular cues for depth perception*

Figure 10.7 *An example of texture gradient*

PERCEPTION OF SIZE

As you watch somebody walking towards you, the image they create on your retina will get larger but they do not appear to grow bigger. Your perception has made adjustments to the sensory information so the person appears to be the same size. This is called **size constancy**.

In Figure 10. 8 the further figure appears larger in the left-hand photograph than she actually is (see right-hand photograph). Why is this? In the first photograph we do not see the woman's size as different from that of the woman in front, rather we see her as being distant from the front woman. The perspective lines in the corridor indicate distance, so our perception **scales up** the image to compensate for the distance.

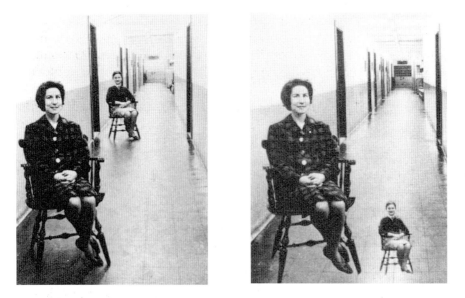

Figure 10.8 *An illustration of size constancy – women sitting in a corridor*

You can test size constancy for yourself by stretching your arms straight out in front of you at shoulder height. Turn up your hands so you can see the back of them. Now, keeping your hands at roughly the same height, bring one hand closer by bending your arm until the hand is about 15 cm from the end of your nose. Look at your hands then shut one eye. Now you can see the difference in size of the retinal image, which your brain automatically 'scaled up' when you looked at your hands with two eyes.

DISTORTIONS OF PERCEIVED SIZE AND DISTANCE

Size constancy does not always occur; if you look at oncoming vehicles through a car windscreen, they do appear to grow much larger in size. The windscreen provides a frame of reference with which your perception compares the changing size of the cars, and the windscreen frame hides some of the clues which would enable size constancy to occur.

The notion of 'scaling up' refers to the idea that 'size' is related to both the size of the object on the retina and to the perceived distance. So, the retinal image of the object is compensated by the brain's calculation of that object's distance away from you. It 'scales up' the retinal image accordingly. This is an explanation for why the moon appears larger when it is close to the horizon. We judge its size in relation to the objects around it – trees and roof tops, for example. We 'scale up' the moon, so it appears larger than when it is high in the sky.

DISTORTIONS OF PERCEIVED MOVEMENT

We perceive that something is moving by comparing it with something else. If you move your finger along this line as you read, you see words disappear and re-appear from behind it, and see the changing position of the finger in relation to the shape of the page. However, we can make errors in our perception of movement. Have you ever sat in a stationary train and seen the train next to you pulling out, only to find that it is your own train which is moving? When there is no sound or sensation of movement from your train you perceive that you are stationary, so you conclude it must be the other train which is moving.

When we are landing in a plane it may seem as though the ground is rushing up to meet the plane, rather than the plane dropping down towards the ground. Certainly it seems as though the ground is moving fast and the plane is barely moving although we know that this cannot be so. This is one reason why pilots use instruments to land their aircraft, rather than the visual information they receive through the cockpit window!

Another example of distortions in our perception of movement occurs when you look at the moon on a windy night. The moon appears to be whizzing through the clouds – although you know it is not! This effect occurs when a small object is surrounded by a larger one which moves. Our perception is that it is the smaller object which moves, not the larger. This is an example of induced movement.

When a small point of light is presented in a totally dark room the light appears to move even though it does not. This is known as the autokinetic effect and was used by Sherif in his study of conformity (see p. 27). One explanation for this is that the eye is continuously making small movements which we are normally unaware of. Because of these movements the position of the image on the retina changes, but it seems as if the brain cannot decide what is causing this movement of the retinal image. Is it the eye which is moving or is it the light? Without a reference point for the light, the brain may come to the wrong conclusion. When a stationary stimulus is presented along with the light, this illusion of movement usually disappears.

FACTORS AFFECTING PERCEPTION

We have already noted several of the ways in which perception is an active process. Below we consider some of the factors which affect our perception, leading us to select certain aspects of it and interpret it in a particular way.

MOTIVATION

When we are hungry or thirsty, psychologists say we are highly motivated to satisfy our need for food or drink. J. Gilchrist and L. Nesburg (1952) studied whether such motivation affects perception. In one condition participants were deprived of food for up to eight hours, in the other condition they were not hungry. In both conditions participants were shown a number of pictures and asked to rate how brightly coloured each one was. Results showed that hungry participants rated the pictures of food as more brightly coloured than the other pictures. When they were not hungry, partici-pants perceived no difference between the food and non-food pictures. We can conclude that motivational state can affect perception.

PERCEPTUAL SET

Perceptual set refers to our tendency to think along certain lines. Perceptual set can be triggered by an image and is then used to interpret ambiguous information. G. Fisher (1967) used the drawings shown in Figure 10.9. Cover up the bottom row of drawings and look at the top row from 1a to 1d. What is 1d? Now look at the bottom row from 2a to 2d. What is 2d?

Fisher found that participants tended to view 1d as a man's face and 2d as a woman's body. In fact 1d and 2d are identical images, but Fisher concluded that because of the sequence in which they have been viewed, our perceptual set leads us to interpret them in a different way.

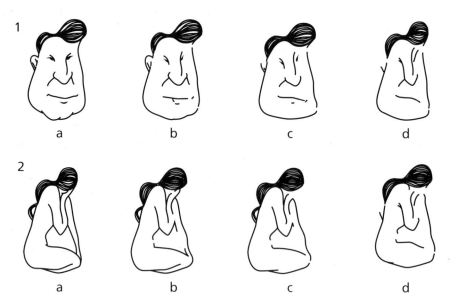

Figure 10.9 *The man/woman ambiguous figure*

EMOTION

C. Solley and G. Haigh (1958) tested whether emotions affect perception by studying children's drawings of an exciting event – Christmas. They asked children to draw pictures of Father Christmas in the weeks before and after Christmas. They found that as Christmas came closer, the pictures became larger and the number of presents increased. In the drawings done after Christmas there were fewer and fewer presents and Father Christmas became smaller and smaller. The conclusion is that emotion affects our perception.

However, this is not an investigation of something seen, rather how it is represented in the mind. The research illustrates some of the difficulties that psychologists have when trying to investigate emotions. They frequently have to use indirect methods and so cannot be sure that they are testing what they actually want to test.

PREVIOUS EXPERIENCE

Previous experience may lead us to misperceive, as demonstrated by Jerome Bruner and Leo Postman (1949). Participants were shown playing cards with the wrong colour suits – black hearts and red spades. These were shown at a very fast rate using a tachistoscope, a machine which allows researchers to present visual images very rapidly and also to vary the speed at which they are presented.

Participants reported seeing red hearts and black spades (which is what they expected to see, based on previous experience). When the cards were displayed at a slower speed, participants reported seeing them as brown or purple. From the results we can conclude that our perception is influenced by our previous experiences and if we have insufficient time to match our expectation with reality, it is our expectation, which dominates. However, when what we see does not match our expectation, but we have insufficient time to verify the real information, it appears that our perception compromises between the two. In this study by Bruner and Postman the compromise produced apparently brown or purple images.

CONTEXT

A. Minturn and J. Bruner (1951) tested the part that context plays in the interpretation of an ambiguous figure (as shown in the centre of Figure 10.10).

In one condition participants were shown the figure with the numbers either side. In the other condition the figure had letters either side. Afterwards participants were asked to reproduce the figure. Results showed that participants who had seen the figure with numbers drew a 13 (exaggerating the space between the 1 and the 3), but those seeing it with letters drew a B (reducing the space).

We can conclude that the ambiguous figure was perceived in terms of the context in which it was seen. This also provides evidence of how we reconstruct memory, a topic discussed on p. 139.

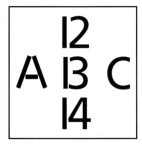

Figure 10.10 *The context for the ambiguous figure*

PERCEPTUAL DEFENCE

Elliot McGinnies (1949) used the term **perceptual defence** to explain why recognition time of emotionally arousing words was slower. He compared the time it took his participants to recognise neutral words (such as broom, apple) and taboo words (such as belly, whore) which he classed as emotionally arousing. The results showed that participants took longer to recognise taboo words, so McGinnies concluded that we show perceptual defence against words which are emotionally arousing.

Critics argued that because taboo words are less familiar they take longer to be recognised. In addition, participants may have been reluctant to report seeing the taboo words. Subsequent research suggested that the delay was probably not due to reluctance to report them. However, research has also found the opposite effect, in which participants recognised taboo words faster.

EVALUATION

Criticism of the studies of factors affecting perception focuses on their **ecological validity** – the degree to which they represent real-life experiences of perception. However, although looking at playing cards on a tachistoscope is not related to real life, there is considerable evidence to suggest that many of these factors do indeed translate to real life.

APPLICATIONS TO EVERYDAY LIFE

The influence of emotion on our perceptions has been exploited in advertising, where advertisers try to create positive emotions (happiness, well-being, humour) when they present their product. An object in an advert (such as a car) will appear more attractive if it is presented in an attractive context.

This ability to match expectation with reality is a skill used in a variety of work settings. For example, a proof-reader checks books or newspapers for printing errors. This requires the rapid matching of previous experience (the correct way to spell a word) with what is being read.

We use some of these techniques to decode handwriting which we find difficult to read. We look at the total sentence to gather meaning, we look at the word length and try to identify recognisable characters and so on. From our previous experience, and the context of the illegible writing, we may be able to correctly perceive the words.

There are implications in this for eyewitness testimony. Our perceptions of an incident are influenced by what we expect to see, by the context in which the incident occurs and our emotional state. For example, if we are frightened we may perceive an attacker to be bigger than he actually is. Imagine that someone witnesses a hold-up in a bank, and the robber says he has a gun and demands money. The witness may 'see' a gun in his hand when all he had was a piece of metal. The context provides the expectation that the object is a gun.

The human tendency to use perceptual set, previous experience and context is not restricted to visual perception. Elsewhere in this book there are discussions of other examples, such as in social scripts (p. 35), memory (p. 135 and 139), and stereotyping (p. 7).

Sample Exam Questions

1 Briefly describe the functions of any two parts of the eye.
   (4 marks)

2 What is the difference between sensation and perception?
   (2 marks)

3 a Identify one visual illusion. *(1 mark)*
   b Provide an explanation for it using your knowledge of psychology. *(3 marks)*

4 Name two monocular depth cues.
   (2 marks)

5 Give an everyday example of a distortion of perceived movement and explain why it occurs.
   (4 marks)

6 Describe one study in which a factor affecting perception was investigated. Indicate in your answer the reason for the study, the method used, the results obtained and conclusions drawn.
   (5 marks)

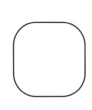

Learning

The way in which psychologists test whether something has been learned is by looking at behaviour. For example, two boys watch a video of a boy damaging toys. Afterwards both boys are given the same type of toys to play with. One child does the same thing as the boy in the video – we say he has learned the behaviour. We know this because we can see him doing the same thing! However, the other child plays with the toys without damaging them. He may have remembered what he saw in the video, and may do the same thing himself in a few days' time, but unless we see him performing the behaviour, we cannot be sure he has learned it.

LEARNING

Learning is the process by which a relatively permanent change in behaviour occurs, which is due to experience. In this chapter we will be examining the work and theories of the behaviourists, who believed that psychologists should only study what is observable, rather than 'memory', 'thoughts' or 'motivation', hence their focus on behaviour.

The first two explanations of learning involve conditioning, and we will also examine ways in which conditioning principles have been used to change human behaviour. The final explanation in the chapter involves social learning, which incorporates cognitive elements such as memory.

CLASSICAL CONDITIONING

Ivan Pavlov, a Russian physiologist, was studying digestion in dogs in the early 1900s. While he was measuring how much saliva the dogs produced in different circumstances, he noted that they began salivating when they heard the researcher's footsteps approaching. Salivation is a reflex response; it occurs automatically when an animal smells food, but Pavlov reasoned that the dogs in his study had learned to associate the sound of footsteps with the arrival of food because the two stimuli had occurred together so many times.

Pavlov tested this learning using the apparatus shown in Figure 11.1. After presenting the food on a dish on many occasions, the dog eventually salivated to the dish alone. Salivation had become **conditioned** to an empty bowl. In further research he presented food at the same time as a stimulus, such as a ringing bell. After several trials, the dog salivated to the bell; its **response** (salivation) had become associated with a new **stimulus** (the bell).

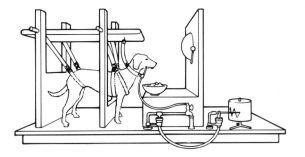

Figure 11.1 *Pavlov's apparatus for studying conditioning with dogs*

In a study which raised ethical concerns, John Watson and Rosalind Raynor (1920) demonstrated the process of **classical conditioning** in an 11-month-old boy. While 'Little Albert' was playing happily with a white rat, a metal bar was struck close to him – this caused the **fear response**. In the fear response the person 'jumps', heart rate increases and other physiological responses occur. After several trials, in which the bar was struck while the child played with the rat, Little Albert became frightened of the rat. When it was given to him he cried and tried to crawl away. In classical conditioning terms a new **stimulus–response link** had been learned.

Thus, through classical conditioning, Albert learned to show the fear response towards an object which, previously, he had not feared. The reflex response (such as fear) is called the **unconditional response** (UCR) because it is not learned. The stimulus which causes fear (the loud noise) is called the **unconditional stimulus** (UCS).

The rat is called the **conditional stimulus** (CS); when the fear response has become associated with the rat it becomes the **conditional response** (CR). The process of classical conditioning is shown in Figure 11.2, using Little Albert's experience as an example.

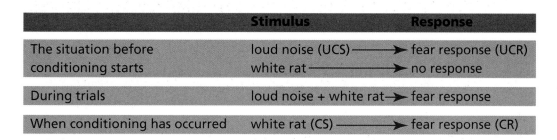

	Stimulus	Response
The situation before conditioning starts	loud noise (UCS) ⟶ white rat ⟶	fear response (UCR) no response
During trials	loud noise + white rat⟶	fear response
When conditioning has occurred	white rat (CS) ⟶	fear response (CR)

Figure 11.2 *The classical conditioning process*

Pavlov and others conducted many studies of classical conditioning, proposing the following principles as a result of their research.

EXTINCTION

Extinction has occurred when the conditional stimulus no longer triggers the conditional response. In other words, Little Albert's fear of the rat could have been unlearned. To do this, Little Albert would be given the rat but there would be no loud noise. Eventually he would no longer show fear when given the rat; his fear response would be extinguished. This is what Watson and Rayner intended to do but the little boy was taken away before they could do so.

SPONTANEOUS RECOVERY

Although the behaviour may become extinct, it is not forgotten. Pavlov found that if, after a delay, the animal was presented with the conditional stimulus (the bell) then it showed the conditional response (salivation) which had, apparently, been extinguished. This is called **spontaneous recovery**.

GENERALISATION

Generalisation occurs when the response is also triggered by a stimulus which is similar to the original one. For instance, Watson and Rayner found that Little Albert was also fearful of a white rabbit and of cotton wool. Pavlov demonstrated that his dogs salivated to bells of a slightly different pitch from that of the one to which they had become conditioned.

DISCRIMINATION

Even though generalisation has occurred, the animal can learn not to generalise. To do this, the unconditional stimulus is presented only with the conditional stimulus. In other words, the dog is given food only when the original bell is sounded. Pavlov found that after several trials the dog only salivated to the original bell – it showed **discrimination**.

OPERANT CONDITIONING

According to the principles of **operant conditioning**, learning occurs as an animal operates in its environment. The animal behaves in an unplanned, random way but the consequences of its behaviour influence whether or not the behaviour will be repeated.

THE LAW OF EFFECT

At about the same time as Pavlov was studying dogs, Edward Thorndike (1898) was studying cats. He found that a hungry cat could learn to open a latch in order to escape from a box and reach some fish which was outside. At first the cat hit the latch accidentally as it was running around the box trying to get to the fish, but every time it was returned to the box there was less time before it opened the latch and escaped. From this type of study Thorndike generated his **Law of Effect** – behaviour which leads to pleasant consequences will become 'stamped in' and behaviour leading to undesirable consequences will be 'stamped out'. The consequences must come soon after the behaviour is performed if learning is to occur.

SKINNER AND OPERANT CONDITIONING

The principles proposed by Thorndike were developed and tested by B. F. Skinner. He devised a Skinner box, which contained a mechanism (such as a lever or a key) for delivering a food pellet to the animal inside. When a rat or a pigeon had been placed in the box, Skinner (1938) noted that having once pressed the lever accidentally and received a food pellet (which was a pleasant consequence), the animal needed less and less time before it pressed the lever again.

Skinner varied his research, for example sometimes no food pellet was delivered, and sometimes the rat was given an electric shock which could be stopped by pressing a lever. From this research he stated that behaviour was shaped and maintained by its consequences, and proposed a number of principles that he claimed were also applicable to humans.

OBJECTIVITY IN RESEARCH

Thorndike, Watson and Skinner represent the behaviourist approach in psychology which focuses on what is observable – behaviour. They contended that most behaviour is learned from the environment, and the laws of learning were similar across species. Therefore results from the study of animal learning could be generalised to humans.

Animals are also easier and cheaper to study than humans and allow for greater objectivity in research. Skinner's box made it possible for him to operationalise independent variables in a precise way and to measure exactly the behaviour which resulted.

Skinner proposed that if the consequences of a behaviour are pleasant, then the behaviour is more likely to be repeated; it is strengthened. If the consequences are unpleasant then the behaviour is less likely to be repeated; it is weakened. It is important to note that we judge whether a consequence is pleasant (or unpleasant) by whether the behaviour is strengthened (or weakened). For fastest learning, the consequences should immediately follow the behaviour and be applied every time the behaviour occurs.

REINFORCEMENT

Reinforcers are consequences which strengthen behaviour. **Reinforcement** (which is the process of strengthening behaviour) functions in two different ways:

- **Positive reinforcement** strengthens behaviour by providing a consequence which the individual finds rewarding. Anything which satisfies a basic human need is called a **primary reinforcer** (such as food or drink). Some psychologists argue that praise is a primary reinforcer, because it satisfies a basic need for approval from others. A gold star, sweets, a hug or money are called **secondary reinforcers** because they do not satisfy basic instincts but are nevertheless pleasant.

- **Negative reinforcement** strengthens behaviour by removing or stopping an unpleasant experience. Rats were given slight electric shocks through the floor of their cage, and a lever in the cage switched off the shocks. To begin with the rat would knock the lever accidentally and the shocks would stop. After several trials the rat learned to press the lever to stop the shocks, which illustrates that behaviour which stops an unpleasant experience is strengthened.

GENERALISATION AND DISCRIMINATION

In operant conditioning the learner will **generalise** by performing reinforced behaviour in similar circumstances. A child who is praised when she is friendly towards visitors will generalise this behaviour to other people. If parents want to stop her being friendly towards complete strangers she meets in the street, they must ensure that she receives praise only when she is friendly to people the parents know. This is an example of **discrimination**.

PARTIAL REINFORCEMENT

If behaviour is not reinforced each time it occurs then it gradually becomes **extinguished**. However, if reinforcement is only applied intermittently, extinction takes much longer. In Skinner's work with rats, if the food pellet was delivered only after the rat had hit the lever three or four times, then after several trials the rat would continue to hit the lever many more times even when it failed to receive the food.

This is called **partial reinforcement**; an animal will maintain its behaviour for longer if it has previously been conditioned using partial reinforcement. An example of partial reinforcement for humans is in gambling, where there is only the occasional win, but the gambler keeps gambling because he knows that at some point there will be another win. This is one reason why slot machines have flashing lights and make lots of noise when a player wins – this acts as reinforcement for players at other machines.

BEHAVIOUR SHAPING

Reinforcement can be used to create completely new behaviour by shaping random behaviour and building up a sequence of behaviours. Skinner demonstrated this by teaching pigeons to play ping-pong. He provided reinforcement every time a pigeon showed behaviour which was close to what he wanted, such as providing food when a pigeon moved towards the ball. Once that behaviour was established, reinforcement was withdrawn and only provided when the animal touched the ball. By reinforcing a narrower and narrower range of behaviours, the pigeon would eventually go to the ball and hit it with its beak.

The use of behaviour shaping with humans is described below under Behaviour Modification (p. 128).

PUNISHMENT

A **punisher** is any consequence which weakens behaviour. Punishment can be, for example, a parent shouting at a child for being rude. If the child becomes less rude, then shouting has acted as punishment. If, however, the child continues to be rude, it may be because being shouted at was rewarding. If the child wanted parental attention, then being shouted at is pleasant and thus strengthens the child's behaviour. This underlines the importance of looking at what the consequences mean to the individual. Punishment can also be in the form of a withdrawal of something desirable. The child may be banned from watching TV for a day, or the parent may behave coldly for a while. This is known as love withdrawal and is discussed further under Moral Behaviour, p. 72.

Skinner claimed that punishment has a limited effect in weakening behaviour because it only weakens a particular response. A two-year-old may stop hitting her newborn baby brother when she is punished, but may start hitting the dog. Punishment does not show what the undesirable behaviour should be replaced with. In contrast, positive reinforcement shows which behaviour is desirable. Skinner recommended rewarding the right behaviour rather than punishing the wrong behaviour.
To summarise, the three consequences which affect behaviour according to operant conditioning principles are:

- a **positive reinforcer** strengthens behaviour – because it is pleasant
- a **negative reinforcer** strengthens behaviour – because it stops something unpleasant
- **punishment** weakens behaviour – because it is unpleasant.

Punishment and negative reinforcement are often confused, but as you can see above, they are very different. Essentially punishment is anything that weakens behaviour whereas negative reinforcement is anything that strengthens behaviour.

Classical and operant conditioning are similar in that both are types of associative learning. Also, generalisation, discrimination, extinction and spontaneous recovery occur in both. However, there are differences, which are summarised in Table 11.1 below.

	Classical conditioning	**Operant conditioning**
What behaviour can be conditioned?	reflexive, automatic	random, voluntary
Why does learning occur?	two stimuli have been presented together	because of consequences of behaviour
How certain is behaviour?	stimulus always produces response	behaviour probable but not certain
Can new behaviour be created?	no	yes

Table 11.1 *Differences between classical and operant conditioning*

APPLYING CONDITIONING PROCEDURES TO HUMAN BEHAVIOUR

We have already seen some examples of both classical and operant conditioning which may be used to change children's behaviour. They have also been used to extinguish behaviours which are damaging for the individual, such as phobias or anorexia, as well as to encourage new behaviours. Some examples are described below.

BEHAVIOUR THERAPY – THE USE OF CLASSICAL CONDITIONING

This treatment is based on the principle that behaviour (such as fear or alcoholism) is a response to a stimulus. Treatment requires the extinction of that response, as outlined in the three methods described below.

SYSTEMATIC DESENSITISATION

A phobia is a **fear response** to a stimulus such as a person, animal, object or situation. In **systematic desensitisation** the person with the phobia (the phobic) is exposed very gradually to the feared stimulus.

- To begin with, the phobic and the therapist together create a hierarchy of fear. This is a list of increasingly fearful situations, starting with one that the phobic can tolerate and ending with one which would create the most intense fear. Using the example of fear of spiders (arachnaphobia), this list may start with a photograph of a house spider which is put on a table, then the phobic picks up the photograph, then touches the image of the spider and so on, until the most intense situation might be having a real spider on his skin.
- The phobic is taught relaxation techniques and when completely relaxed, the phobic experiences the first stage of the hierarchy of fearful situations (looking at the photo). When they are comfortable with that level of exposure, they move to the next stage. Again, the phobic is relaxed and then experiences the next stage of exposure.
- The phobic does not move to the next fearful situation until they feel ready. If they become fearful treatment returns to the previous stage. Finally they are able to handle the most feared situation comfortably. The phobia is extinguished.

This method is thought to work because it seems unlikely that humans can be in two opposing states (fear and relaxation) at the same time. Therefore the stimulus (the spider) cannot trigger the phobic response (fear). However this is undermined by work with very young children. It is not possible to teach them relaxation techniques, yet phobias have been extinguished using gradual exposure without relaxation.

Figure 11.3 *Someone who is fearful of spiders may be able to do this after treatment using either systematic desensitisation or flooding*

Systematic desensitisation is generally successful in treating specific phobias (of an animal or an object), but is less so for more general phobias such as fear of open spaces (agoraphobia). It is more suitable for use with children than the techniques described below. Ethical concerns are few, because the patient plays such an active part in the structure and pace of the treatment. However this too can be problematic because the treatment may take an extended period of time and the phobic may fail to complete it if she feels she is not progressing.

IMPLOSION/FLOODING

Implosion or **flooding** are also examples of techniques to treat phobias, and they are based on the idea that the human body cannot maintain the **fear response** for a prolonged period. In contrast to the previous method, the phobic is confronted with her most intense fearful situation. Implosion requires the phobic to imagine the most fearful situation; in flooding it is actually experienced. The procedure for flooding is as follows.

- The phobic is exposed to the feared stimulus (a spider on the arm, being in the middle of a large supermarket, looking out over the top of a tall building). The phobic experiences an intense fear response.
- This situation is maintained, the phobic cannot escape and the response continues. The phobic may show intense mental and physical distress.
- Eventually the response becomes exhausted because the body cannot maintain that level of physiological arousal. So the phobic is in the feared situation but does not show the fear response, as it has become extinguished.

The evidence suggests that these techniques, particularly flooding, are the most successful. They are quicker and cheaper than systematic desensitisation. However, they do raise ethical concerns, as the therapist takes considerable responsibility for the phobic's well-being. They may have to act against the wishes of the phobic, as expressed during the flooding.

However, before the phobic takes part the full procedure and the phobic's likely response should be explained. Usually the phobic is given time to think about the treatment before they decide to go ahead with it. This is why these techniques are not appropriate for children, who cannot fully understand how they will feel, nor be in a position to give informed consent.

AVERSION THERAPY

This aims to stop behaviour by conditioning it to something unpleasant. Aversion therapy has been used to treat alcoholics, using the **classical conditioning** procedure as illustrated below.

- The alcoholic is given a drug which causes nausea (which is a reflex response over which the individual has no control).
- The patient is then given a drink of alcohol and the drug, so the two are paired together.
- This pairing occurs several times until the alcohol (the conditional stimulus) becomes associated with nausea (the conditional response), so the patient no longer drinks alcohol.

The success rate for aversion therapy is uneven. It seems to be more effective for some people than others. One difficulty is that if the pairing does not continue occasionally, the association will become **extinguished** and the alcoholic may return to drink. The only way to avoid this is for the alcoholic to stay away from alcohol.

Figure 11.4 *Situations such as this are difficult for a former alcoholic who has undergone aversion therapy*

There are ethical concerns in this method because of the effects on the patient and the responsibility on the therapist. As in the previous method, the alcoholic is given very detailed information about what the treatment entails and what they might experience. Usually they are given time to think about this before they decide to have the treatment, and may need ongoing support if it is to be successful.

BEHAVIOUR MODIFICATION – THE USE OF OPERANT CONDITIONING

Behaviour modification uses the principle of **reinforcement** to change behaviour, as you will see from the two applications described below.

BEHAVIOUR SHAPING
Behaviour shaping has been used to elicit new, more desirable behaviour. We saw how Skinner used it to teach pigeons to play ping-pong but in humans it has helped improve the communication skills of autistic children, as described below.

- The therapist first identifies an activity which the child enjoys, such as playing with a special toy, or using the swing.
- Every time the child looks at the therapist she gives him the toy to play with.
- Eventually the child looks at the therapist in anticipation of the toy but she withholds it until the child reaches for the toy.
- Every time he reaches for the toy, he is given it as the therapist says 'please'.

- When reaching has become established, the toy is withheld until the child himself makes a sound as he reaches, then he is given the toy.
- This continues, reinforcing a behaviour and then withholding reinforcement until a more specific behaviour has become established. If the technique is successful, the child may eventually speak spontaneously.

This has been found to be an effective technique, but reinforcement usually needs to be maintained in order for the child to continue the behaviour.

TOKEN ECONOMY

The principle here is that desired behaviour is rewarded with tokens which can be exchanged for something which the individual wants. The token economy is used mostly in institutional settings such as psychiatric hospitals, where a fixed tariff is awarded for behaviours such as taking a shower (perhaps five tokens) and tokens can then be used to buy desired rewards (perhaps ten tokens to watch a video).

This has been found to be very effective for managing patients and improving their self-care and social skills. However, it requires close monitoring of patient behaviour for it to work, and patients tend to become very dependent on the system, making it difficult for them once they leave the institution.

THE USE OF CONDITIONING PROCEDURES

We have looked at some applications of conditioning, and noted their strengths and weaknesses. But there is a more general criticism about this work which is important. Even though behaviour is changed, the underlying causes of that behaviour are not addressed. As a result, a new kind of maladaptive behaviour may emerge. It also fails to take sufficient account of the individual's understanding, motivations or emotions. This is linked to another point – some of these techniques allow vulnerable people to be controlled by those who are more powerful, and this power may be abused.

SOCIAL LEARNING

The key feature of social learning is that learning occurs through the processes of **observation**, **imitation** and **reinforcement**.

OBSERVATION

We learn by observing others. Those who are observed are called **models** because they are modelling behaviour which is imitated. Bandura, a leading social learning theorist, proposed that children are more likely to imitate models who are important to them because they are:

- **similar** (perhaps the same sex or age)
- **powerful** (such as a parent, teacher or pop star)
- **caring** (such as a parent, relative or teacher)
- **rewarded** for their behaviour (such as gaining approval for being aggressive); this is known as **vicarious reinforcement**.

As a child develops, different models become more or less important; a three-year-old girl will imitate the behaviour of her mother whereas a 14-year-old girl might imitate a pop star.

IMITATION

A child imitates the behaviour of the model who has been observed. So a little girl observes her mother's behaviour when she scrapes her knee. Later the child makes her teddy have an accident, then sticks a plaster on his knee, cuddles and consoles him just like her mother did to her.

The principles of social learning emerged from research on aggression carried out by Bandura and his colleagues (1961) which is described in detail under Anti-social Behaviour (pp. 98–100). In this work, Bandura noted that although some children did not imitate behaviour they had nevertheless observed it. He found that when children were offered a small reward for reproducing behaviour they had seen, almost all could do so, even though they had not produced it spontaneously when they had the opportunity.

DESCRIBING RESEARCH

In order to describe research in an exam question you will need to be able to do the following:

Give the reason why the study was conducted, the method used, the results obtained and the conclusions drawn.

Practice doing this with one of Bandura's experiments which are described on pp. 98–99.

REINFORCEMENT

If a child imitates a model's behaviour and the consequences are rewarding, the child is likely to continue performing the behaviour. If a parent overhears the little girl consoling her teddy bear and says 'what a kind girl you are', this is rewarding for the child and makes it more likely that she will repeat the behaviour. Her behaviour has been **reinforced**. As we have seen, we do not imitate everything we observe. This may be because:

- the models are not important to us; for example Bandura found that boys are less likely to imitate a female model showing aggression than a male model showing aggression.
- the behaviour is not appropriate in that setting; a child may learn that certain behaviours are approved of (rewarded) by his friends but not by his parents.
- we have seen that the model's behaviour had unpleasant consequences. Bandura found that children were less aggressive if they saw a model punished for aggression, so if a boy sees his football hero sent off the pitch amidst boos and jeers, he is unlikely to imitate the behaviour which got the player sent off.

Observational learning is more complex than conditioning because the individual has to see what is done, hear what is said, remember all of this and then be able to reproduce it some time later. All of these are **cognitive** processes. As the child gets older he is able to notice, remember and reproduce more complex behaviour.

Slowly, through reinforcement, the child will **internalise** a model's behaviours so that it will be able to act as the model would act in a situation it has never seen the model in. For example, our little girl with her teddy bear would console other children when they were hurt even if no-one was watching. This is an example of how social learning theory would explain the development of pro-social behaviour.

Sample Exam Questions

1 Define
   a 'spontaneous recovery' *(2 marks)*
   b 'discrimination'. *(2 marks)*

2 What is meant by the Law of Effect?
   (2 marks)

3 Using your knowledge of psychology explain what is meant by 'punishment'.
   (5 marks)

4 Identify one similarity and one difference between classical and operant conditioning.
   (2 marks)

5 Describe a conditioning procedure which a psychologist might use to help a child overcome a fear of birds.
   (5 marks)

6 Describe the part which imitation plays in social learning theory.
   (4 marks)

CHAPTER

12

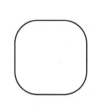

Memory

Without memory we would be unable to do many of the things we take for granted: to use words, to dress ourselves, to recognise a familiar voice, even to recognise our own face in the mirror. Without memory, everything we experience would seem to be experienced for the first time; it would be completely new to us. This chapter provides three explanations for memory, considers reasons why we forget and reviews some applications for the results of memory research.

MEMORY

When you are watching a film your brain has to process the information you receive from it. The images you see enter your eyes as light waves, and what you hear enters your ears as sound waves. In order that you can make use of it, this information is:

- **Encoded** – the information is changed (or encoded) so that it can be stored.
- **Stored** – information is stored, and is available for use at some time in the future. We store different types of information in different ways, and the way we store information affects how we retrieve it.
- **Retrieved** – this occurs when we try to recover information from storage. If we 'can't remember' something, it may be because we are unable to retrieve it.

One of the first psychologists (William James, 1890) distinguished between two types of memory; these are called **short term memory** and **long term memory**. This distinction forms the basis for much of the research on memory, so we will now look at encoding, storage and retrieval as they relate to both short term and long term memory.

ENCODING

Incoming information is changed (or encoded) so that it can be stored. How do you remember a telephone number you have looked up in the phone book? If you can 'see' it then you are using visual coding, but if you start repeating it to yourself you are using acoustic coding (by sound). Evidence that we often use acoustic coding comes from research by R. Conrad (1964) who showed a list of six consonants (such as BKSJLR) to participants. The list was shown only briefly, and participants were then asked to write down the consonants. When they made a mistake, it was usually because they wrote down a consonant which sounded like one they had seen, such as 'P' instead of 'B'. This suggests that information is coded acoustically in short term memory.

Alan Baddeley (1966) conducted a similar study but used four sets of words. He wanted to test acoustic memory (by sound) and semantic memory (by meaning). He tested short term memory by asking participants to recall the words immediately after seeing them, and tested long term memory by having a delay before participants recalled them. The types of words and participants' success in recalling them is shown in Table 12.1 below.

Type of words	Short term memory test	Long term memory test
Acoustically similar (e.g. man, cap, can)	poorer recall	similar recall in both sets
Acoustically dissimilar (e.g. pit, few, cow)	better recall	
Semantically similar (e.g. great, large, big)	similar recall in both sets	poorer recall
Semantically dissimilar (e.g. good, huge, hot)		better recall

Table 12.1 *Showing the types of words and success in recall in Baddeley's (1966) research*

Baddeley concluded that coding in short term memory is mainly acoustic but in long term memory it is more likely to be semantic (by meaning). However, you will see throughout this chapter that information in long term memory is encoded in other ways as well, such as visually or acoustically.

STORAGE

Most adults can only store between 5 and 9 items in short term memory. It is as though we have about 7 (plus or minus 2) 'slots' in our short term memory and once they are filled any more new information pushes out, or displaces, the information already there. Although short term memory seems very limited, research has shown that if we 'chunk' information together we can store more.

G. Bower and F. Springston (1970) tested the effects of 'chunking' in an experiment using two groups of participants. The control group was presented with groups of letters such as: FB, IPH, DTW, AIB, M. The experimental group was given the same letters but grouped differently: FBI, PHD, TWA, IBM. You can see that when arranged like this, the letters 'make sense' to us so we automatically 'chunk' them. The experimental group recalled many more letters than the control group, and the researchers concluded that 'chunking' increases the capacity of short term memory. To 'chunk' like this we must use information from long term memory.

It seems that information can be stored for only a brief period in short term memory. In research by L. Peterson and M. Peterson (1959), participants were presented with trigrams (such as XPJ, AKM). However, to prevent them from trying to remember the trigrams by repeating them, they were asked to count backwards, out loud, in threes from a particular number. They were tested after several seconds, and the results showed that after three seconds recall was 80 per cent correct, but after longer delays it gradually deteriorated until after 18 seconds it was only 10 per cent. The conclusion is that information in short term memory fades rapidly unless it is repeated (or rehearsed).

In contrast, long term memory can last a lifetime, and its capacity is vast. Some of the evidence related to long term memory is described later in this chapter, particularly the work by Murdock (p. 136), Bartlett (p. 139) and Loftus (p. 143).

RETRIEVAL

When we are asked to retrieve information from memory, the differences between short and long term memory become very clear. If participants are given a list of numbers to remember and then asked what is the number before '4', participants go through the list in the order they heard it in order to find the answer. This shows that information is stored sequentially in short term memory, and this is also how it is retrieved.

In long term memory, information is stored by association. This is why you can remember what you went upstairs for if you go back to the room where you first thought about it. The context of this thought (the room) is associated with the thought itself. Two ways in which information is associated in long term memory are discussed below. You will see that they can be used in everyday situations to aid recall, and may be particularly useful when revising for examinations.

ORGANISATION

G. Bower and his colleagues (1969) gave participants words to remember. The experimental group saw the words arranged in a **hierarchical** fashion according to meaning (see Figure 12.1) The control group saw the words arranged randomly in a list. Those in

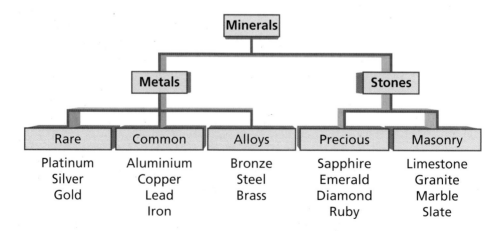

Figure 12.1 *Words arranged in a hierarchy, as used in Bower's (1969) experiment*

the experimental group recalled 65 per cent of the words, whilst those seeing the random list recalled 19 per cent. It appears that organising material makes it easier to recall.

Material can be organised in a sequence (such as alphabetically, or by size or by time) to aid recall. Imagine a patient discharged from hospital whose treatment involved taking various pills at different times, changing a dressing and doing exercises. If the doctor gives these instructions in the order in which they must be carried out through the day, this will help the patient remember them.

CONTEXT

As we noted above, retrieval of information can be improved when it is related to context. D. Godden and A. Baddeley (1975) asked deep-sea divers to memorise a list of words. One group did this on a beach and the other group were five metres under water. When they were asked to remember the words the groups were divided. Half the 'beach' learners remained on the beach but the rest had to recall under water. Half the 'under-water' learners remained there but the other half had to recall on the beach. The results showed that those who recalled in the same environment as that in which they had learned the words recalled 40 per cent more than those recalling in a different environment. This suggests that retrieval of information is improved if it occurs in the context in which it was learned.

You can can use this technique when taking an exam, by shutting your eyes and imagining yourself back in your classroom, or where you did your revising. Putting yourself back in this context should help your recall. The role of context is discussed further on pages 144–145 under Eyewitness Testimony.

THREE EXPLANATIONS OF MEMORY

Now that we have reviewed some aspects of memory, we will look at three approaches to the understanding of memory.

THE MULTISTORE MODEL

Richard Atkinson and Richard Shiffrin (1968) proposed that memory can be thought of as a process. Information passes through a series of stores, each of which has different characteristics. At the start of the process, we pay attention to some of the information which is registered by the senses and this is held briefly in the sensory memory store. This passes into short term memory and then on to long term memory. Details of how the information is processed are described below and illustrated in Figure 12.2.

- **Sensory memory** – this stores information for only a few seconds and in its original form (speech is stored as sounds, visual information as images). If it is encoded it will pass into short term memory, but if it is not, then the sensory information fades.
- **Short term memory** – information which has been encoded passes into short term memory. We have already looked at the characteristics of short term memory, noting that information can be maintained if it is rehearsed.
- **Long term memory** – information may then transfer from short to long term memory because of rehearsal or through the process of encoding, where it may

remain indefinitely and can be retrieved for future use. Encoding in long term memory may be visual, acoustic or semantic (by meaning). In principle, long term memory has unlimited capacity, but information may be lost for a variety of reasons which are discussed shortly.

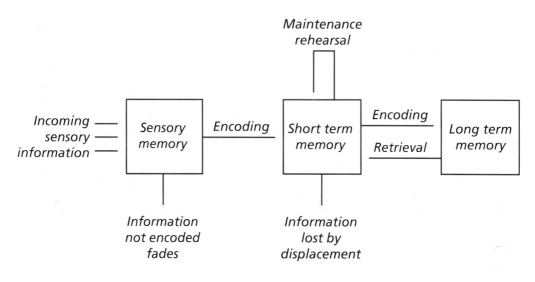

Figure 12.2 *Atkinson and Shiffrin's multistore model of memory*

There is considerable research to support this model. For example, studies of **amnesia** in brain-damaged patients, which are described under Forgetting (p. 142), suggest that amnesia may be due to difficulties transferring recently acquired information into long term store.

The distinction between short and long term memory is illustrated in **free recall** experiments, such as those by B. Murdock (1962). He gave participants a number of words to remember and then asked them to recall as many as possible, in any order. The first words to be recalled were those the participants heard last (the **recency effect**) and this is evidence that the last few words were still stored in short term memory.

The other words recalled were those heard first (the **primacy effect**). Murdock concluded that these words were stored in long term memory, because the participant has the opportunity to rehearse the first few words. Few of the words from the middle of the list were recalled, perhaps because either they were not fully registered (and therefore decayed) or there was lack of time to rehearse them as effectively as the first words, so they did not pass from short to long term memory.

EVALUATION OF THE MULTISTORE MODEL

Although the multistore model does provide a simple description of memory processes and research supports the characteristics of short and long term memory described above, this has been widely criticised for its focus on memory for new facts, such as word lists, numbers or nonsense syllables. This is why the model seems to explain how we remember a telephone number until we can dial it, but it cannot explain many of our everyday experiences of memory. For instance, why are we able to recall information which we did not rehearse yet be unable to recall information which we have rehearsed? Why can we remember how to swim, which is not learned as 'pieces' of information? Why could you read this page several times and yet recall very little of it?

Figure 12.3 *Does Atkinson and Shiffrin's (1968) model explain how this surfer remembers his skills?*

The model also requires interaction between long term memory and sensory memory. For example, we use our long term memory in order to recognise that the sounds which enter sensory memory are words. The model cannot satisfactorily explain how we do this. When participants are questioned about their experiences in the free recall experiments they often describe the strategies they use to try to remember, and their other thoughts whilst hearing the words. So other **cognitive** factors such as attention and memory strategies are important.

LEVELS OF PROCESSING APPROACH

Fergus Craik and Robert Lockhart (1972) proposed a different way of interpreting the evidence that short and long term memory are two different stores. They claimed that whether or not we remember depends on what we do with the information that comes in. For example, remembering a phone number by **acoustic** rehearsal (that is, by repeating it to yourself) does not involve thinking about it very deeply. In other words, it is processed at a **shallow level**, and this is why it is quickly forgotten. In contrast, if you tried to remember the number by elaborating on it – perhaps linking it to other familiar numbers or seeing patterns in the numbers – you are processing this information more deeply and are therefore more likely to recall it. They propose that memory is therefore a by-product of the **depth of processing** of information and there is no clear distinction between short and long term memory.

To test this theory, F. Craik and E. Tulving (1975) told participants that their experiment was about testing speed of perception and reaction. They presented them with a word, very rapidly, then a question about the word (examples of the questions are listed in Table 12.2 below). Some questions required participants to process the word in a shallow way, others in a deep way. Then participants were given a long list of words and asked which they had already seen during the experiment.

The words that required participants to think about the meaning were more likely to be recognised than those relating to their appearance. Table 12.1 gives the results of the research. These suggest that the more deeply the material is processed the more likely it is to be remembered.

Level of processing required	Question asked	Words recognised later
Structural level (appearance)	'Is the word in upper case letters?'	18%
Phonetic level (sound)	'Does the word rhyme with...?'	50%
Semantic level (meaning)	'Does the word go in this sentence?'	80%

Table 12.2 *Results of Craik and Tulving's experiment*

EVALUATION OF THE LEVELS OF PROCESSING EXPLANATION

Although this approach can also explain much of the evidence on memory reviewed so far, there are criticisms as well. In particular:

- Words which require deeper processing also require more effort to process; it could be the extra effort which increases remembering.
- Deeper processing also takes more time, and it could be this which increases remembering.
- The model does not explain why deeper processing helps memory. Michael Eysenck (1979) proposed that the material used to test for shallow processing is not **distinctive**, which is why it is not recalled so well. Better recall may therefore be due to distinctiveness.

These criticisms underline a more general point, which is that the explanation describes but fails to explain memory. Nevertheless, this explanation is useful in everyday life because it highlights the way in which elaboration, which requires deeper processing of information, can aid memory. Three examples of this are:

- **Reworking** – putting the information in your own words or talking about it with someone else.
- **Method of loci** – when trying to remember a list of items, linking each with a familiar place or route. In order to remember a shopping list, for example, you could imagine your route to the shops and create an image of each item, such as bread going in the bank, tomatoes at the traffic lights, sugar in the school play-

ground. You are processing the information more deeply and organising an otherwise unconnected list of words.

- **Imagery** – by creating an image of something you want to remember, you elaborate on it and encode it visually. This is a technique sometimes used by people learning a foreign language. They think of an English word which sounds like the foreign word they are trying to learn, and then find a way of linking them together. Figure 12.4 shows two examples of words you could use when learning French.

Five is 'CINQ' (pronounced sank)   Wine is 'VIN' (pronounced van)

Figure 12.4 *Examples of the use of imagery when learning French*

CONSTRUCTIVE APPROACH

F. Bartlett (1932) saw memory as an active process, not a stored copy of something. He proposed that we use existing knowledge to understand new information and impose meaning on it. These points are illustrated in his famous 'War of the Ghosts' research. This is a North American folk story, an excerpt of which is shown below in Figure 12.5, and it was given to participants to read.

Over varying periods, from a few hours to several months, participants were asked to recall everything they could about the story. Bartlett found that they imposed their own meaning on it. In particular they:

- omitted some details and added new details
- gave reasons for incidents
- added emphasis to some parts
- changed the order of incidents.

Bartlett concluded that people 'reconstructed' their memories and the changes noted above are ways in which we try to make sense of information, and we may distort it in the process.

Barlett called our existing understanding a schema. A **schema** provides us with information about what to expect, and helps us to fill in the gaps when information is incomplete. An example of a schema is a stereotype, which is a ready-made expectation of what someone is like because they belong to a particular group. This topic is discussed more in Chapter 1, pp. 7–11.

One night two young men from Egulac went down the river to hunt seals, and while they were there it became foggy and calm. Then they heard war-cries, and they thought: 'Maybe this is a war-party.' They escaped to the shore, and hid behind a log. Now canoes came up, and they heard the noise of paddles, and saw one canoe coming up to them. There were five men in the canoe, and they said:

'What do you think? We wish to take you along. We are going up the river to make war on the people.'

One of the young men went, but the other returned home. And the warriors went on up the river to a town and they began to fight, and many were killed. But presently the young man heard one of the warriors say:

'Quick, let us go home: that Indian has been hit.' Now he thought: 'Oh, they are ghosts.' He did not feel sick, but they said he had been shot.

Figure 12.5 *An extract from Bartlett's 'War of the Ghosts' story*

EVALUATION OF THE CONSTRUCTIVE APPROACH

This approach cannot be tested rigorously because of the difficulty of comparing what individual participants each remember at different times. Some criticism has been directed at the story, which was ambiguous and not similar to everyday experience. Researchers who asked participants to recollect their own real-life experiences found that each time they were asked, their recollections were very similar.

However, the constructive explanation does relate to our everyday use of memory. Because it stresses the extent to which we impose our own meaning on material, particularly when there are gaps or ambiguities, it has important implications in situations where accurate recall is crucial. One example is eyewitness testimony, which we explore at the end of this chapter.

We have looked at three explanations of memory, and these are compared in Table 12.3 on page 141.

EXPLANATIONS OF FORGETTING

There are many reasons why we 'forget', although it is difficult to test them because we may not in fact forget, we may simply be unable to retrieve the memory from storage at a particular time. Four explanations of forgetting are discussed below.

INTERFERENCE THEORY

Our memory may be hampered by information we have already stored, or by new experiences which occur whilst we are taking in the information. There are two types of interference:

	Multistore model	Levels of processing	Constructive
Is memory explained/described?	explained	described	explained
Long term storage of information is due to	maintenance rehearsal	by-product of deeper processing	fitted into already existing understanding
How is memory studied?	lists of sounds/words	processing words in various ways	events/descriptions
Are studies objective?	yes	yes, but difficult to draw conclusions	no
How much of everyday memory does it explain?	not much	quite a lot	quite a lot

Table 12.3 *Summary of comparisons between different explanations of memory*

- **Retroactive interference** occurs when information you have received recently inter-feres with your ability to recall something you learned earlier. B. Underwood and L. Postman (1960) tested this by asking participants to learn a list of paired words (such as cat–tree, jelly–moss, book–tractor). Half of the participants (the experimen-tal group) then learned a second list (such as cat–glass, jelly–time, book–revolver). You can see that in the second list the first word of each pair is the same, but the second word is different. The control group were not given this second list. All par-ticipants were then asked to recall the words in the first list. The researchers found that recall in the control group, who only learned the first list, was more accurate than in the experimental group. This suggests that learning the items in the second list interfered with participants' ability to recall the first list. This is an example of retroactive interfence.
- **Proactive interference** occurs when something you already know interferes with your ability to take in new information. This was demonstrated using a similar procedure. The experimental group learned both lists of word pairs but the control group learned only the second list. Recall was better in the control group.

Interference theory has been criticised because it is based on laboratory experiments requiring participants to remember words. This is a rather artificial test of forgetting so the results may not reflect real life, though it may explain why people find it difficult to learn two similar languages.

MOTIVATED FORGETTING

Sigmund Freud (1901) proposed that when we find an experience very distressing we push it down into our unconscious so that we cannot access it. Freud called this **repres-sion**; it helps us cope with the strong emotional feelings which the memory creates.

Psychoanalytic techniques such as dream interpretation can be used to access repressed memories but they may produce quite distressing feelings in the individual, which raises **ethical** concerns. If the individual is very upset by these memories, they may be buried so deeply that they cannot be accessed, so researchers cannot actually discover whether or not they are really forgotten.

An alternative explanation for failure to remember unpleasant experiences is that when we are emotionally aroused, perhaps very fearful, our bodily responses change and these changes may interfere with our cognitive abilities. E. Loftus and H. Burns (1982) showed participants a film of a bank robbery, but the experimental group saw a violent version in which someone was shot in the face. When tested later, the experimental group had poorer recall of details in the film than the control group. It can be concluded that fear can damage memory, though it is not clear whether the participants failed to notice details, or noticed them but failed to retain them. There are also, of course, ethical concerns with research such as this.

AMNESIA

Amnesia refers to loss of memory due to brain damage, perhaps because of a blow on the head, a stroke or infection. There are two types of memory loss:

- **Anterograde amnesia** is the inability to learn and store new memories after a brain injury. The memory may be retained for a short time but it does not appear to 'sink in'; to be stored in long term memory. However, the amnesia may be due to the patient's inability to retrieve new information which is stored in long term memory. Memories stored before the injury can be recalled.
- **Retrograde amnesia** refers to the loss of memory for events before the injury. The loss may be extensive, particularly with severe injury, or quite brief. Yarnell and Lynch (1973) studied American footballers who suffered concussion during a game. Their research showed that the footballers could recall what had happened as soon as they gained consciousness. However, when asked twenty minutes later to describe what had happened, they were unable to do so. Yarnell and Lynch concluded that the information had not been transferred from short term to long term memory. A possible reason for this is discussed in the next section.

Brain injury can cause amnesia for many reasons but there is still much we do not know about the brain so it is difficult to explain what causes amnesia in each case. In addition, because the research uses **case studies**, psychologists must be very cautious in drawing general conclusions from them. Nevertheless, where patients with similar types of injury also have similar memory problems, this enables psychologists to focus more closely on particular parts of the brain, their functions and how they may be linked together to affect memory.

TRACE DECAY THEORY

According to this theory, information is forgotten as time passes. The memory trace involves tiny changes in the brain, and if the memory is to be retained this trace must be strengthened, which is what happens in rehearsal. Unless it is strengthened the trace decays; it breaks down and fades. This is an explanation for loss in short term memory and may explain the American footballers' amnesia, described above. It has also been used to explain some long term memory loss, insofar as lack of use of information in long term memory may also lead to decay of the memory trace.

In an experiment to test whether decay was due to the passage of time or to inter-ference from other factors, J. Jenkins and K. Dallenbach (1924) asked participants to learn a list of nonsense syllables. Some participants learned them in the evening and went to sleep afterwards. The other group learned them in the morning and then continued with their normal activities. They were tested after one, two, four and eight hours, and the results showed that although recall decreased in both groups over the first two hours, in the active group it was poorer, and continued to deteriorate until after eight hours it was almost non-existent. In contrast, the sleeping group were still able to recall on average five syllables after eight hours.

The researchers concluded that forgetting may be due to decay but also to interef-erence, in this case **retroactive interference** (see p. 141). In terms of everyday applications, this suggests that if you want to remember something, then learn it just before you go to sleep!

Trace decay theory is a possible explanation for re-learning. Sometimes we think we have forgotten something, perhaps how to do something on a computer. Then someone shows us what to do, and after only one demonstration we can remember the whole sequence. This is called re-learning; it is as if going through something just once or twice strengthens a memory that had started to decay.

EYEWITNESS TESTIMONY

Memory research has been able to help evaluate the accuracy of reports by people who witness an accident or a crime. Elizabeth Loftus is one of a number of psychologists who have argued that eyewitness testimony in court is very unreliable. In a series of studies she investigated whether people reconstruct events, whether reconstructed memory persists and whether they can be 'led' to remember something which they did not see.

E. Loftus and J. Palmer (1974) showed participants several films of car accidents and after each one they were questioned about the accidents. Results showed that participants' estimates depended on whether the cars were described as 'hitting' or 'smashing' into each other. Subsequently Loftus and Palmer extended this research to discover whether participants' reconstructed memory persisted.

> **INDEPENDENT AND DEPENDENT VARIABLES**
> In Chapter 13 there are explanations of independent and dependent variables. Use this information to give the IV and the DV in the Loftus and Palmer experiment described below.

Participants were divided into three groups and all saw a film of a traffic accident and were then asked questions. One group's question referred to the cars 'hitting', for another group they 'smashed' and in the third group (the **control group**) this question was not asked at all. A week later they all answered several more questions, including whether they had seen broken glass, although there was no broken glass in the film. The results are shown in Table 12.4.

	'Smashed'	'Hit'	Control group
Mean estimated speed (after seeing the film)	10.5 mph	8.0 mph	
Participants reporting broken glass (one week later)	32%	14%	12%

Table 12.4 *Estimated speeds and answers to 'broken glass' question*

These results demonstrate Bartlett's proposal for the **reconstructive** nature of memory and of its persistence. Importantly, it shows how changing the wording of a question can affect memory.

FACTORS AFFECTING THE RELIABILITY OF EYEWITNESS TESTIMONY

LEADING QUESTIONS
The evidence provided by Loftus and Palmer's research shows how the choice of words affected the judgements that participants gave. This is an example of the way leading questions can influence the account of an eyewitness, as well as distorting their long term memory for an event.

EMOTION
Our emotional state may affect our ability to recall information. The research by Loftus and Burns (see p. 142) showed poorer recall in participants who had seen a more violent version of a bank robbery. In a study of a real-life event, D. Wright (1993) asked participants to recall details of the 1989 Hillsborough football disaster. He found that five months later they could not remember very much, and this memory deteriorated over time. This evidence suggests that witnessing emotionally arousing events may indeed lead to poorer memory.

CONTEXT OF QUESTIONING
We have already seen in the research with deep-sea divers by Godden and Baddeley (see p. 135) that recall of information is better if it is linked to the person's situation when they were first storing it. Research on memory has contributed to changes in police procedures for interviewing eyewitnesses. R. Geiselman and colleagues (1985) have developed the **cognitive interview**, which aims at enhancing eyewitness recall. Police are now advised to do the following:

- Help the eyewitness try to create a similar context by imagining what he was wearing, and his mental state.
- Ask the eyewitness to describe the sequence of events from before the event so as to build the context more thoroughly. This relates to the way information is organised in memory (see pp. 134–135).
- The eyewitness is encouraged to describe what he has seen from another perspective ('What would you have seen if you had been standing at the opposite corner?').
- Rather than interrupt the eyewitness for details, police ask about a newly recalled item when it is recalled because this uses the person's own recall context.
- Allow time between questions, in case the account given by the eyewitness triggers further details.

Recall may, of course, be enhanced if the eyewitness revisits the scene of the crime. This is the purpose of the crime reconstructions which are broadcast in TV programmes such as *Crimewatch*. The hope is that this will trigger recall more effectively than merely describing an event or asking if anyone was in the area at a specific date and time.

Figure 12.6 *Revisiting the scene of a crime can enhance recall*

PHYSIOLOGICAL AROUSAL

As we saw under Forgetting, arousal due to strong emotions such as fear or anger can disrupt cognitive processes and damage memory (see pp. 141–142). One way of increasing the eyewitness's ability to recall information would be to return them back to the same emotional state. Clearly there are **ethical** concerns in encouraging someone to become greatly distressed for this purpose.

FACE RECOGNITION

Research has suggested that people are rather poor at recognising the face of a stranger. An eyewitness is likely to stereotype, so the memory will be influenced by what she thinks a criminal looks like. When we stereotype we interpret ambiguous information in terms of the stereotype. This is an example of the constructive nature of memory (see p. 139), and is discussed further in Chapter 10, Perception.

Research shows that we seem to look at the face as a whole rather than particular features. Indeed face recognition seems to involve a part of the brain which is not used in general object recognition. This makes it more difficult for an eyewitness to construct a face using the 'Identikit' method, which builds faces feature by feature. In addition, the Identikit face is fixed whereas the features of real people are constantly moving.

Our ability to recognise faces when they are moving and showing emotion was studied by V. Bruce and T. Valentine (1988). Lights were attached to a face which was then filmed in the dark. Participants who saw the film were able to identify the facial expressions, such as frowning, and could sometimes identify the person on the basis of the movements alone. This evidence suggests that humans are able to recognise a face as a whole rather than as a number of features.

The police may therefore use an artist to draw the face that an eyewitness describes. The artist is able to illustrate descriptions like 'a threatening sort of face' and incorporate elements such as emotional expressions.

You can see from these five factors how some of the points we have covered in this chapter can affect eyewitness testimony.

Sample Exam Questions

1 a In psychology, what does the term 'encoding' refer to? *(2 marks)*
  b Describe one study in which encoding has been investigated. *(5 marks)*

2 Briefly outline the 'levels of processing' explanation of memory.
  (5 marks)

3 From what you know of psychology, explain why elaboration of information can aid recall.
  (4 marks)

4 a Identify two psychological explanations for forgetting. *(2 marks)*
  b Describe one study in which forgetting has been investigated. *(5 marks)*

5 Discuss one way in which the research on memory can be used in everyday life.
  (3 marks)

6 Use psychological evidence to discuss one way in which the accuracy of eyewitness testimony might be improved.
  (5 marks)

Methods of Investigation

Hugh Coolican (1995) says there are three major ways in which psychologists get information about people – 'you ask them, watch them or meddle.' This chapter describes the ways in which psychologists ask, watch and meddle. In other words, we are going to look at research methods. Some of them permit a high degree of control, others are devised to study how people behave naturally, some generate information which is easy to count (or quantify) whereas others focus more on experience. We also consider how to choose the most appropriate method, variables and ways of measuring behaviour.

SCIENTIFIC METHODS

The scientific method involves gathering information, studying it to identify patterns or relationships, generating theories to explain these patterns and then devising a hypothesis in order to test the theory. The hypothesis must be tested in a controlled and objective way, so the results of the test provide evidence to support or refute the hypothesis.

The method employed to test the hypothesis should be objective, standardised, replicable and value free. The closest the researcher can get to achieving these aims is to use a laboratory experiment, because of the high level of control it provides. B. F. Skinner's research on operant conditioning in animals is a good example. However, as you will see in the descriptions below, the gain in objectivity achieved by a laboratory experiment may bring weaknesses with it.

HYPOTHESES

A **hypothesis** is a precise and testable statement of what the researcher predicts will be the outcome of the study. In an experiment this is called the experimental hypothesis and an example would be 'Participants sitting alone will respond faster to a call for help than participants sitting with two others.'

In a **correlational study** (for details see p. 153) the hypothesis is called a research hypothesis, and it will predict a relationship between two variables. For example,

'There will be a correlation between the number of people in a group and the level of conformity shown by an individual.'

Every hypothesis also has a null hypothesis. This predicts that there will not be a difference; that any difference is due to chance. For example, 'There will be no difference between a participant alone and sitting with two others in the time taken to respond to a call for help. Any difference will be due to chance.' In the correlational study the null hypothesis would be 'There will be no correlation between the number of people in a group and the level of conformity shown by an individual. Any correlation will be due to chance.'

Essentially, the two hypotheses cover the possible outcomes of the research. When the results have been analysed, they should tell the researcher which hypothesis can be retained and the other will be rejected.

INDEPENDENT AND DEPENDENT VARIABLES

As we have already noted, the experiment gives researchers greater control over what happens and enables them to test cause and effect. The researcher keeps all variables constant except the one they are investigating (which is the **independent variable**), and then measures what effect this has on another variable (called the **dependent variable**).

In an experiment to test the hypothesis we have just devised, the independent variable (IV) is the number of people present with the participant and the dependent variable (DV) is the time taken to call for help. This is a straightforward way of measuring the dependent variable but measuring behaviour is often more complex. Zimbardo (p. 33) used the level of electric shock given by the participant as the measure of aggression.

CONTROLLING VARIABLES

To be confident that the IV has indeed caused the DV, the researcher must control all other aspects of the experiment, that is, the other variables. Some variables which researchers need to consider are:

- **Situational variables** – these are aspects of the environment which may affect the participants' behaviour in the experiment, such as variations in the light, the time of day, the way instructions are given or background noise. Situational variables should be controlled so they are the same for all participants.
- **Participant variables** – this refers to the ways in which each participant differs from the others, and how this could affect the results. For example, if participants doing a word memory task were tired, dyslexic or had poor eyesight, this could affect their performance and the results. Researchers try to ensure that such variables are evenly distributed between the research groups. How they do this is described under Experimental Design on page 155.

METHODS OF INVESTIGATION

Each method of investigation has a general type of procedure, as described below. When psychologists plan research they choose the method which is most appropriate to what they are investigating.

EXPERIMENT

As we noted above, an experiment involves the manipulation of the independent variable to see what effect it has on the dependent variable. Although we also referred to control of variables, in reality psychologists never have full control of all the variables. The topic of control is covered in more detail in Chapter 14; below we will briefly refer to control as we consider four different types of experiment.

LABORATORY EXPERIMENT

In the laboratory experiment there is a high level of control because researchers can isolate cause and effect by controlling other variables. The psychologist decides where the experiment will take place, at what time, with which participants, in what circumstances and using a standardised procedure. It is easier to replicate the laboratory experiment. An example is Conrad's research on acoustic coding (p. 132).

Nevertheless, the laboratory experiment has weaknesses, for example the artificiality of the setting may produce unnatural behaviour that does not generalise to real life, and **demand characteristics** may also bias the results (see p. 158).

FIELD EXPERIMENT

In a field experiment the psychologist manipulates the IV but the experiment takes place in a real-life setting, so there is less control over variables such as the people who take part or when the study happens. This may bias the results as well as make the experiment more difficult to replicate. Piliavin's 'subway' study of bystander intervention is an example (p. 90).

However, participants' behaviour in the field experiment is more likely to reflect real life because of its natural setting, and because there is less likelihood of demand characteristics affecting the results.

QUASI OR NATURAL EXPERIMENT

The quasi or natural experiment is one in which the IV occurs in real life so the researcher cannot 'create' a difference for the purpose of the experiment. In the quasi experiment the IVs may be age, gender or race. In the natural experiment the IV is already occurring. An example is Hodges and Tizard's (1989) research which compared the long term development of children who had been adopted, fostered or returned to their mothers with a control group of children who had spent all their lives in their biological families.

SURVEY

A survey asks people questions, either through face-to-face interviews or written questionnaires. The questions must be carefully prepared so that they are clear, and do not persuade the respondents (the people answering the questions) to answer in a particular way. The researcher might first conduct a pilot study with the questions, giving them to a few people and asking for comments. If the questions are unclear or produce biased answers, the researcher can adjust them for the main study.

In order to reduce demand characteristics (see p. 158) which might encourage participants to give the answers they think the researcher wants, a survey may be given a general title such as 'A study of children's toys' – when it is actually trying to find out whether parents encourage their children to play with toys related to their gender. In addition, a few questions may be included which give the impression the survey is about something else, perhaps asking how much the parent spends on toys or the child's attitude to books. Answers to these questions are noted but not counted as data.

The questions may be closed or open-ended, depending on the kind of information the researcher wants:

- **Closed questions** produce clear-cut answers which are easy to interpret and quantify, such as 'Is your child happy at school? – yes/no?'. Respondents may want to answer 'Well, it depends', yet because they are forced to choose yes or no, their answer will not reflect their real opinions. A compromise is the question which provides a range of answers, perhaps using a scale from 1 to 5 to reflect the strength or amount of agreement. This provides more detailed information which is still easy to quantify.
- **Open-ended questions** give the respondent the opportunity to provide a lot of information and is useful for in-depth research, for example 'What do you think of your child's school?'. However, it is difficult to compare different people's answers, so the open-ended question is less useful when trying to quantify information.

QUESTIONNAIRES

Because they require written answers, questionnaires depend on respondents being able to read and understand correctly. They may be distributed by hand, by post or from a distribution point such as a doctor's surgery or supermarket. Once completed they can be returned by post or collected by hand. The researcher has no control over how accurately or thoughtfully people answer the questions, whether they understand them correctly or indeed whether they return the questionnaires at all.

Questions can be closed or open-ended but must be clear, unambiguous and understandable. Respondents should remain anonymous, so they must not be asked to give their names.

Questionnaires are quick and easy to operate if they use closed questions. A very large sample can be used and people who are geographically distant can be studied. However there are disadvantages in that the sample will be biased because it relies on people returning the questionnaires (they may be returned by people who have plenty of time or strong feelings about the topic). Respondents may not give accurate answers due, perhaps, to misunderstanding or boredom.

INTERVIEWS

Here the researcher asks the questions face-to-face but this may encourage people to give the kind of answers they think the interviewer wants, or to give **socially desirable** answers. The structure of the interview can vary:

- **Structured interviews** consist of a series of fixed questions with a limited range of possible answers, much like a questionnaire. They are the fastest to complete and if well prepared they provide data which is easy to quantify and analyse. However, they do suffer the drawbacks of closed questions.

- **Semi-structured interviews** comprise open-ended questions which cover the information the researcher wants to gain. However, respondents may provide this information without being asked a specific question, so the researcher is flexible about the questions themselves, and the order in which they are asked. This style is useful for gaining more in-depth and accurate information from respondents, but it is more difficult to compare answers.
- **Clinical interviews** are the most informal and in-depth technique. They enable the interviewer to rephrase questions if necessary, to ask follow-up questions or clarify answers that are ambiguous or contradictory. This technique was used by Piaget in his work with children (see Chapter 5) and may be used to diagnose mental disorders. Although it provides detailed information, this should not be generalised to the population as a whole, and it is possible that the interviewer may bias the response or misinterpret answers which are given.

OBSERVATIONS

When psychologists observe, they watch people's behaviour and measure particular aspects in a way which is as precise as possible. It is usual to have more than one observer because behaviour is complex and the observer may be biased. If the behaviour is videoed, the observers will analyse the behaviour from the video. They need to be trained in how to analyse and measure the behaviour being studied so that they all interpret it in the same way. This is called **inter-observer reliability**.

Behaviour is noted on an **observation schedule**. The researchers must decide what behaviours are to be noted. This is quite complex, for instance measures of aggression might involve pushing, kicking, various facial expressions and shouting. Decisions must be made about how the participants will be observed and over what time period. Observers may watch a child for a full playgroup session or they may observe a child for five minutes every 15 minutes. This is called **time sampling**. If they are interested in behaviour in a particular setting, they will observe children in that setting, such as any child who comes to play in the sand box.

The behaviour may be analysed by being broken down into units, for example the behaviours shown in Figure 13.1. Here the observer would note each time a child performed one of these behaviours. The observer may have categories of behaviour on the schedule, such as playing alone, playing with one other, playing in a group, interacting with an adult. The task here would be to categorise the behaviour and note how much time is spent performing that particular behaviour.

Researchers may run a **pilot study** because they can then watch the kind of behaviour they will be analysing, and thus devise the most useful measures. Figure 13.1 shows a simple schedule for observation of co-operation in children's play: each participant is identified by a number in order to preserve **confidentiality** (see Ethics, p. 159).

The observational method can be used for a variety of purposes, as described below.

NATURALISTIC OBSERVATION

Here the researchers have no control. They look at behaviour which occurs naturally in the participant's own environment, such as a school playground. Before starting the study, the observers try to become familiar to those they are observing in order to minimise the effect that their presence may have on them.

Participant number	Number of times participant performed action				
	gave object	smiled at other	physically assisted other	agreed to help	encouraged other
P1					
P2					
P3					
P4					

Figure 13.1 *Example of an observation of co-operation in children's play*

It is valuable to see how people behave in a natural setting and an observation provides very detailed information which can be used as a starting point for further, more controlled, research. It can be used when other methods might be unethical. However, the presence of observers could influence the behaviour of those being observed and it is difficult for observers to be completely objective. This can be an expensive and time-consuming way of gathering and analysing data, and because there are so many variables which could affect behaviour it is not possible to draw any firm conclusions.

CONTROLLED OBSERVATION

This type of observation is frequently used with children or in social psychology research, and may be one of several methods used in the same investigation. In order that control can be exerted and to make behaviour easier to observe (such as through two-way mirrors), the observations may take place in an artificial setting such as a research laboratory. One example is Bandura's study of observational learning and aggression (p. 98).

By controlling some variables, it is possible for the researchers to draw conclusions from their observations, but the unfamiliar setting may affect participants' behaviour, making it less natural. There are also ethical issues relating to informed consent and privacy.

PARTICIPANT OBSERVATION

Here the observer becomes one of the group of people that he or she wishes to observe. The observer may tell the others that they will be observed, or may pretend to be one of the group and not inform them that they are being observed. This method raises particular ethical issues, such as observing people in private, perhaps hearing personal or confidential information and not gaining people's consent to be part of an investigation.

This method does allow researchers to observe people in a natural setting and also to gain some understanding of the causes of their behaviour. It is particularly useful for studying the way people behave when they are in groups. However, the observer may be unable to make notes until they are away from the group, there may be difficulties remembering accurately, or the observer may interpret or record information in a biased way. If the others in the group know they are being observed this may affect their behaviour so it is less natural.

CASE STUDY

The case study is an in-depth study of one person or a small number of people. It may include interviews (using open-ended questions) of the person being studied as well as others who can provide information about the person's past or present experiences and behaviours. Data provided by school or medical records may also be gathered. Because of the detail they provide, they may suggest insights to the psychologist and ideas for further work. Freud used case studies of his patients to devise and generate his theories, as did Bowlby.

The case study gives a detailed picture of the individual and helps in discovering how a person's past may be related to the present. It can be useful in treating individual problems and by studying those who are unusual, psychologists can discover more about what is usual. It does rely on participants telling the truth, and on memory, which may be poor or distorted. Records may be inaccurate or incomplete and the interviewer may be biased towards what they expect to find. Although the information gained about one person cannot be **generalised** to others, the case study can form the basis for future research.

CORRELATIONAL STUDY

Sometimes psychologists want to find out what behaviours go together, for example to see whether the amount of violent television watched is related to the amount of aggression shown. Both the variables may already be occurring, but in order to find out if they are related the psychologist must measure the variables and then calculate a correlation. The data may have come from questionnaires or observations, for example.

There are two patterns of correlation:

- a **positive correlation** occurs when one variable increases as the other increases
- a **negative correlation** occurs when one variable increases as the other decreases.

It is important to remember that a correlational study can only show a **relationship** between two variables; we cannot assume that one variable causes the other. It is one way of gaining more information about variables which cannot be controlled and enables us to predict the value of one variable from the other one. It can be used when it would be unethical to conduct an experiment, for example to see whether there is a correlation between the security of a child's attachment and their level of disobedience, and may form the basis for a follow-up study to test cause and effect.

EXERCISES

Using the material in this book, find your own example for each method of investigation described in this chapter.

CHAPTER

14

Methods of Control

In order to reduce the many extraneous variables which could influence the results of an investigation, there is a range of methods by which the researcher can exert control. This chapter considers ways in which the researcher can increase control over the research environment, and so have greater confidence in the results which emerge.

SAMPLING

The participants in research, the sample, should be as representative as possible of the target population. This target population may be six-year-olds, male adults, parents, insecurely attached children or witnesses of crime. To ensure representation there are several ways of choosing participants. The more representative the sample, the more confident the researcher can be that the results can be **generalised** to the target population. Having said this, very few samples in research are truly representative, as you will see from the following descriptions of sampling methods.

RANDOM SAMPLING

Be warned, this is not what you think it is. Random sampling is highly controlled! It means that every member of the target population has an equal chance of being selected. For instance, in a study with a target population of seven-year-olds, the names of seven-year-olds from different types of primary schools (inner city, suburban, private, and so on) would be gathered. These children would provide the sampling frame.

Each child must have an equal chance of being selected, so the names of all the children may be written on a slip of paper, put in a box or bag and mixed up. To select 20 participants, the first 20 names taken out of the box would comprise the sample. Alternatively, each child may be given a number and the sample selected using the above method, a random number table or computer-generated randomisation.

OPPORTUNITY SAMPLING

Researchers rarely use random sampling; they have to rely on participants who are more easily accessible. For example, a psychologist wishing to study pre-school children may use the children who are attending the university creche and who fit the criteria for age, sex and so on. This is an example of opportunity sampling: it is quick and cheap in comparison with other methods. Anyone who is available, and agrees to take part in research, can become a participant.

Opportunity sampling occurs in field experiments such as Piliavin's (1969) New York subway studies. However, they are unlikely to be a representative sample. Selecting names from a telephone directory is another example of opportunity sampling, but this is not a representative sample because many people are not listed in a directory, and some do not have phones.

SELF-SELECTED SAMPLING

A self-selected sample is one where participants have offered to take part, for example people who return questionnaires or surveys, or who have volunteered by responding to advertisements in newspapers or on the radio. Research has shown that these people are unlikely to be representative of the population, for instance they may be more outspoken, have more spare time or have strong feelings about the topic being researched.

STRATIFIED SAMPLING

A stratified sample is one which is in proportion, in the relevant characteristics, to the target population. This is also called **quota sampling**. Imagine you are conducting a survey of women to ask questions about their attitude to childcare. You need to find out what proportion of females in the population fall into categories such as: self-employed, working class, professional, unemployed, married, divorced, single, 20–30 years old, 30–40 years old and so on.

You can get this information from census data, which might show, for example, that 10 per cent of females are self-employed and 20 per cent are working class. You select people on the basis that they fit into these categories until you have filled your quota, so that 10 per cent of your sample are self-employed, 20 per cent are working class, and so on.

EXPERIMENTAL DESIGN

In an **experiment**, data is compared from two (or sometimes more) groups. Sometimes one group experiences the independent variable (called the experimental group) and the other group does not (this is the control group). The way in which participants are assigned to groups is called the **experimental design**. The three types of experimental design are described below.

INDEPENDENT MEASURES DESIGN

Here there are different participants in each group. In quasi and natural experiments the groups are naturally occurring, so participants can only go into one of the two groups. In laboratory and some field experiments the researcher is able to choose which participants are assigned to the experimental group and which to the control group. For details of these types of experiments, see page 149.

This should be done by random allocation, which ensures that each participant has an equal chance of being assigned to one group or the other (for details of randomising, see Random Sampling on p. 154).

However, people vary in their experiences, attitudes, intelligence, alertness, moods – these are participant variables. Because participants are assigned randomly, the researchers do not know, for example, whether one group comprises most of the more alert or skilled participants. If this was the case, these participant variables may produce differences between the results from the two groups which are not due to the independent variable. A large sample is needed to reduce this effect.

The independent measures design is also known as the independent groups design. It is the quickest and easiest way of allocating participants to groups and there are no order effects (which occur with **repeated measures**, see below).

REPEATED MEASURES DESIGN

Here every participant goes through both experiences, which are called the experimental condition and the control condition. This is an advantage, because as the same people are in both conditions there are no participant variables. However, there are drawbacks to this design which might produce biased results. For instance, the participant may guess the aim of the study when they take part in the second condition, so **demand characteristics** may affect the results. Also, because participants may become more skilled, or bored or tired after they have experienced one condition this may affect their performance on the second condition. These are called **order effects** or practice effects.

COUNTERBALANCING

To combat order effects the researcher counterbalances the order of the conditions for the participants. The sample is split into two; one half does the experimental condition (A) then the control condition (B); the other half does the control condition (B) then the experimental condition (A). This is called the ABBA design. Although order effects occur for each participant, because they occur equally in both groups, they balance each other out in the results.

MATCHED PAIRS DESIGN

This design deals with the drawbacks of both the previous designs. It reduces participant variables by matching participants in pairs on the basis of variables relevant to the study, such as age, gender, intelligence, reading ability or socioeconomic background. This may require pre-tests in order to ensure good matching, then one of each pair is randomly assigned to the experimental condition and the other to the control condition. The perfect matched pairs design is one which uses identical twins, assigning one to each condition.

Because participants only experience one condition of the experiment, there are no order effects and so counterbalancing is not necessary. However, this method can be more expensive and time consuming than the others and of course participant variables may still affect the results.

STANDARDISATION

Another way in which control can be exercised is by ensuring that all participants undergo the same experiences. Essentially this means ensuring that they are all given identical instructions in exactly the same way, as described below.

STANDARDISED PROCEDURES

To ensure that all participants have the same experience, researchers should ensure that they are all tested:

- in the same place, with the same equipment and materials placed in the same way
- under the same conditions, so the level of lighting, noise and heat remains the same for all participants
- at roughly the same time of day, as people may behave differently if tested at nine o'clock in the morning rather than five o'clock at night.

STANDARDISED INSTRUCTIONS

Participants should be given identical instructions in exactly the same way. This is particularly important if the research requires performing a task which must be demonstrated. Sometimes the instructions are written down and participants are asked to read them. This eliminates any possible bias which may creep in if they were spoken, but some participants may have difficulty reading or understanding the instructions. For this reason any instructions must be simple, clear and unambiguous.

OBJECTIVITY IN MEASURING AND RECORDING

The point of doing research is to produce data from which conclusions can be drawn. This raises questions for psychologists such as how to measure people's behaviour or attitudes. Observational studies raise issues of measuring behaviour objectively which are discussed in detail in Chapter 13, p. 151. Essentially, there should be several observers who are trained to identify and correctly rate the behaviours being measured.

In interviews or questionnaires, questions should be tested so that they will not lead to biased responses. Answers to questions may be structured, so that they can be directly comparable. For example, responses in semi-structured of clinical interviews may need to be interpreted before they can be compared with others and conclusions drawn. Any data which requires such interpretation is open to bias, though this can be reduced if interpretations are made by two or three independent assessors.

RESEARCH IN NATURAL AND EXPERIMENTAL SETTINGS

The methods outlined in Chapter 13 discuss research in both natural and experimental settings. Examples of natural settings are:

- **field experiments** – in which the researcher manipulates the independent variable but the research itself takes place in an everyday setting
- **natural experiments** – in which the independent variable occurs naturally and research investigates the IV as it already exists
- **naturalistic observation** – in which participants are observed as they go about their ordinary business.

In a natural setting people are more likely to behave in a normal way, but because the researchers are not able to control all the variables, they must interpret the results with caution. There are also ethical issues of consent and privacy.

However, because the researcher is unable to exert control over the setting, it is possible that these uncontrolled factors, or things which are hidden, lead to an incorrect, or at least incomplete, recording of data. Although the setting is natural, participants may not behave naturally if they know they are being studied.

If research takes place in an experimental setting it is much easier to control variables and many of the techniques available to researchers have been discussed in the first part of this chapter. The drawback of the experimental setting is that it may seem very artificial to the participants, perhaps intimidating them so they are more co-operative and obedient than they would be in a natural setting.

Another drawback to the experimental setting is **demand characteristics**. These are any features of the research which may affect participants' behaviour, making them act unnaturally or look for cues to tell them what the research is about and behave accordingly. Being in a strange setting, and being treated in a rather formal, impersonal way by researchers, reminds the participant that something artificial is going on. One way of reducing demand characteristics in the laboratory is to conduct the experiment without the participants realising it. This is what Latané and Darley (1968) did in their smoke-filled room studies (see p. 87).

The artificial nature of the laboratory setting raises the question of **ecological validity**. Because results are generated from a situation which is unlike everyday life, to what extent can the conclusions be generalised to everyday life?

Clearly, there are strengths and weaknesses in both the natural and the experimental setting. Researchers should choose the setting, and method, which is most appropriate for what they are investigating and be mindful of the weaknessses of their chosen method when drawing conclusions from the results.

Ethical Considerations

Ethics are the desirable standards of behaviour we use towards others. If we behave ethically, then we treat others with respect and concern for their well-being. We do not take advantage of their trust or their lack of knowledge. Psychologists have legal and moral responsibilities to those who help them in their research – every individual has rights, and these must be respected and protected. Ethical concerns apply to animals as well, but our concern here is for humans.

ETHICAL GUIDELINES

Participants in research put their trust in the researchers. If they betray the participants' trust this discredits the profession and makes it less likely that others will agree to participate in research in the future. The British Psychological Society has therefore published guidelines specifying **ethical concerns** and how they must be addressed. These guidelines apply to anyone working within psychology, so this includes students of psychology. Some of the most important ethical concerns are described below.

THE INVASION OF PERSONAL PRIVACY

The **privacy** of participants must be protected. This includes confidentiality, observations and the right to withdrawal if participants feel uncomfortable.

CONFIDENTIALITY
Participants, and the data gained from them, must be kept **anonymous** unless they give their full consent. If participants initially agree, and then decide to withdraw that agreement at the end of the study or after they have been **debriefed**, all data and information about them must be deleted from the research. It must not be possible to identify participants from any reporting of the research, such as in an academic journal or a newspaper article. See the observation schedule (Figure 13.1, page 152).

OBSERVATIONS
If participants are observed in public, in circumstances where anyone could observe them, privacy is not an issue. Having said this, if this observer is obvious to those being watched, perhaps taking notes, this may cause **discomfort** or **distress**, which is not acceptable. However, when observers are hidden then privacy is violated and this contravenes the BPS guidelines.

WITHDRAWAL

Even when participants agree to take part, they do not know the extent to which you will encroach upon their feelings, emotions or sense of what is appropriate. This is why researchers must gain **informed consent** (see below) and also tell participants that they can **withdraw** at any time during the research if they wish to do so. Participants should be reminded of their right to withdraw if it is a long study or if they appear to be **distressed**. By reminding them of the right to withdraw you are stressing that they are under no obligation and can act to protect themselves at any time if they feel uncomfortable.

MINIMISING DISTRESS AND DECEPTION

DISTRESS

Researchers must ensure that those taking part in research will not be caused distress. They must be protected from physical and mental harm. This means that you must not embarrass, upset, frighten, offend or harm participants. For example if your study involved showing participants gruesome pictures, this could upset them. This is also an issue in **cross-cultural** research – for example a question asked may offend the **norms** of one culture but not another.

DECEPTION

Deception is sometimes necessary in order to avoid **demand characteristics** affecting the results, but participants must be deceived as little as possible, and any deception must not cause distress. If you have gained participants' informed consent by deception then they will have agreed to take part without knowing what they were consenting to. The true nature of the research should be revealed at the earliest possible opportunity, or at least during debriefing. If the participant is likely to object or be distressed once they discover the true nature of the research at debriefing, then the study is unacceptable.

   If serious deception has been involved the researcher must ensure that the participant understands why and feels comfortable about their part in the research.

INFORMED CONSENT AND DEBRIEFING

INFORMED CONSENT

Before the study begins the researcher must outline to the participant what the research entails, and then ask if they **consent** to take part. If the participants are children, someone who is responsible for them (a parent or guardian) must be told what is involved, and they must give consent. Having gained this, the researcher must still ask the child if they are willing to take part, and the child must agree.

   However, it is not always possible to gain informed consent. This is acceptable as long as what happens to the participants is something which could just as easily happen to them in everyday life. For example, if research involves observing people in a bus queue, those people may be observed by anyone when they are in the queue.

DEBRIEFING

Participants must be thoroughly debriefed at the end of the study. They must be given a general idea of what the researcher was investigating and why, and their part in the research should be explained. They must be told if they have been deceived and it must be justified to them. They must be asked if they have any questions and these should be answered honestly and as fully as possible.

Participants may have experienced distress through their experience, perhaps when they hear they have been deceived or if the procedure caused them anxiety, embarrassment or loss of self-esteem. It is the researcher's responsibility to check on the participants' physical and psychological well-being as part of the debriefing process. If necessary, they should be followed up to ensure there are no ill-effects later on.

SUMMARY

It is sometimes difficult to plan research within these guidelines. Most research requires some degree of deception, for example. Nevertheless, many psychologists have devised clever ways of running studies which are within these guidelines; others have not. You can see that some of the research reported in this book contravenes the guidelines, possibly because the research took place before the guidelines became so strict.

As a student carrying out research for your practical exercise, you must check with your teacher that you are competent to carry out the research. You must ensure that your practical exercise is designed and conducted within these guidelines, and that the way you answer your examination questions shows that you understand and respect them.

Glossary

accommodation	modifying a schema or creating a new one in order to cope with new information (Piaget)
altruism	behaviour which puts someone's well-being before your own, perhaps in a way which is damaging to yourself, without thought of reward
assimilation	using a schema to act on the environment (Piaget)
attachment	a close emotional bond between two people
audience effects	the effects that the presence of others have on the performance of a task
autonomous morality	morals based on one's own rules and taking account of intent (Piaget)
behaviourist	relating to the view that behaviour can be best understood by studying only that which can be observed
bystander behaviour/ intervention	the way in which people who witness an incident behave
case study	a detailed study of an individual's (or a small group's) background
categorisation	grouping things together on the basis of some similarity
central trait	a personality trait which affects the way we assess other personality traits
centration	taking account of only one feature of a situation (Piaget)
child-rearing style	the way parents bring up children
classical conditioning	a form of learning in which an automatic response becomes associated with a previously unrelated stimulus
classification	grouping things according to a particular criterion
clinical interview	a way of finding out about a participant's thinking or emotions by using their replies to determine what questions will be asked next, using open-ended, unstructured questions
concrete operational stage	third stage of cognitive development (Piaget)
conditional response	the response which occurs when the conditional stimulus is presented
conditional stimulus	the stimulus which is presented with the unconditional stimulus
conditions	the experiences which different groups of participants undergo
confederate	someone who appears to be a participant but who is actually part of the study

cognition	anything to do with mental processes such as remembering or thinking
conformity	yielding to the ideas or behaviour of others
conscience	the part of the superego which stops us from doing things we know to be wrong (Freud)
conservation	the understanding that something stays the same even though its appearance changes (Piaget)
control condition/ control group	the group of participants who do not experience the IV
counterbalancing	giving half the participants the experimental condition first and the other participants the control condition first
correlation	a relationship between two variables
correlational study	a study to discover if there is a relationship between two variables
cross-cultural research	research which compares people from different cultures
debriefing	giving a general explanation of the study to participants when they have finished and ensuring their well-being
decentre	to be able to take into account more than one feature of a situation at a time (Piaget)
deindividuation	a state in which the individual becomes less aware of themselves and has less sense of personal responsibility for their own behaviour
demand characteristics	the clues in an experiment which lead participants to think they know what the researcher is looking for
dependent variable	the outcome of manipulation of the indpendent variable; the results
deprivation	loss of or damage to an attachment
diffusion of responsibility	the more bystanders that witness an incident, the less likely it is that one of them will help
distress syndrome	pattern of behaviours shown by children separated from an attached figure
ecological validity	the degree to which an investigation represents real-life experiences
ego	the part of personality in touch with reality (Freud)
ego ideal	the part of the superego that represents what we would like to be (Freud)
egocentrism	seeing the world from only one's own perspective; understanding the world as an extension of oneself (Piaget)
empathy	the ability to match one's own feelings with those of another person
equilibration	being in a state of cognitive balance (Piaget)
ethics	desirable standards of behaviour towards others

ethology	the study of animals in their natural environment
experiment	a research method in which all variables are controlled except one, so that the effect of that variable can be measured
experimental condition/ experimental group	the group of participants who experience the IV
extinction	when a response to a stimulus is no longer seen
field experiment	an experiment which takes place in an everyday environment
formal operational stage	fourth stage of cognitive development (Piaget)
frustration–aggression hypothesis	the proposal that frustration always leads to aggression
gender	the psychological or cultural aspects of maleness or femaleness
gender identity	the individual's understanding of what it means to be male or female
generalise	to apply information from one situation to other situations
halo effect	the tendency to assume that someone with an attractive quality has other positive qualities
heteronomous morality	moral standards imposed from outside the individual and based on the consequences of actions (Piaget)
hypothesis	a prediction of what will happen
identification	the process by which the child comes to take on the ideas and behaviours of the same-sex parent (Freud)
impression formation	making inferences about people on the basis of little information
imitation	copying the behaviour of a model (social learning theory)
independent measures	an experimental design which has different participants in each group
independent variable	what the researcher manipulates
inferential reasoning	thinking about things in the abstract in order to draw conclusions (Piaget)
ingroup/outgroup	the division of people into two groups; the ingroup is the group to which we belong, the outgroup are the others
internalise	to feel that a behaviour or idea is part of us, that we own it
interview	to ask participants questions in a face-to-face setting
learning	a relatively permanent change in behaviour which is due to experience
libido	the life instinct (Freud)

matched pairs	an experimental design in which each group has different participants, but they are paired on the basis of their similarity in several characteristics
maternal deprivation	having no attachment, or a damaged attachment, to the mother (Bowlby)
model	whoever's behaviour the individual imitates (social learning theory)
negative correlation	a relationship between two variables in which one increases as the other decreases
negative reinforcement	anything which strengthens behaviour because it stops an unpleasant experience
norms	the beliefs or expectations which members of a group share
obedience	following the orders of someone else, who may be perceived to be in authority
object permanence	a child's understanding that although it can no longer see an object, the object still exists (Piaget)
observational learning	human learning which takes place by observing others; social learning
observation	research which involves watching and recording behaviour
operant conditioning	learning which occurs as a result of reward or punishment
opportunity sampling	selecting whoever is available to be a participant
outgroup homogeneity	seeing members of the outgroup as more similar than they are
partial reinforcement	reinforcement which follows only some responses; only given once in a while
perception	the process of interpreting, organising and elaborating on sensory information
peripheral traits	personality traits which are affected by central traits
personal construct	the individual patterns we have for interpreting our experiences
phallic stage	the stage of psychosexual development when the libido is focused on the genitals and the Oedipus or Electra conflict occurs (Freud)
pluralistic ignorance	when each bystander takes no action and thus misleads the others into defining the incident as a non-emergency
positive correlation	a relationship between two variables in which one increases as the other increases
positive reinforcement	anything which strengthens behaviour because it is rewarding to the learner

prejudice	an extreme attitude for or against a group, or a member of the group, based on characteristics which are assumed to be common to all members of the group
pre-operational stage	second stage of cognitive development (Piaget)
primacy effect	the first information received has more influence than subsequent information
primary reinforcement	anything which satisfies basic instincts
privation	failure to develop an attachment
pro-social behaviour	behaviour which helps others
psychoanalytic theory	theory based on the idea that behaviour is caused by unconscious forces (Freud)
punishment	anything which weakens behaviour; makes a behaviour less likely to happen
quota sampling	calculating the proportion of particular characteristics in the target population and selecting participants in the same proportions
random sampling	selecting participants on the basis that all members of the target population have an equal chance of being selected
recency effect	later information has more influence than earlier information
reinforcement	anything which strengthens behaviour; makes a response more likely to happen
repeated measures	an experimental design in which the same participants are in each condition
reversibility	the ability to imagine reversing a process
response	the activity which results from a stimulus
role-taking	in a social setting, the ability to take the perspective of someone else
sampling	the method by which participants are selected for research
scapegoating	the process of blaming someone else for your problems
schema	a mental framework comprising what we already know, which we use to understand new experiences and to generate expectations of what is likely to happen
script	a recognised sequence of events which occurs in a social setting
secondary reinforcer	anything which strengthens behaviour but does not satisfy basic instincts
self-efficacy	expectations and feelings of competence about one's abilities
sensitive responsiveness	responding accurately to a baby's needs
sensorimotor stage	first stage of cognitive development (Piaget)

separation anxiety	unhappy response shown by a child when an attached figure leaves
social categorisation	classifying people as members of either the ingroup or the outgroup
social desirability	the wish to be seen by others in a positive way
social facilitation	the change in performance which occurs when performing a task in the presence of others
social identity	the sense of who we are which is gained from membership of a group
social learning	human learning which takes place by observing others; observational learning
social loafing	putting less effort into a task which is being performed with others
social norms	the behaviours and beliefs which an individual is expected to show because of their social role or membership of a group
standardise	to make consistent so that results are comparable
standardised instructions	the identical instructions given to each participant in a study
stereotype	a rigid, generalised and simplified set of ideas about the characteristics of all members of a group
stereotyping	categorising someone as a member of a particular group and assuming they have the characteristics which all members of that group are thought to have
stimulus	anything (such as an event, object or person) which results in a change in someone's behaviour
stranger fear	distress shown by a child when a stranger approaches
superego	the part of personality related to morals, to what we know is wrong, and to the kind of person we want to be (Freud)
survey	a way of gathering information by asking many people to answer standardised questions
symbolic thinking	the use of signs, words or symbols to represent things
thanatos	human instinct for self-destruction (Freud)
trial	a repetition or practice
unconditional response	behaviour over which one has no control, which is automatic
unconditional stimulus	anything which causes an unconditional response
valid	refers to whether a measurement or test does the job it was designed to do
variable	anything which varies
vicarious reinforcement	learning from the way others are reinforced

Further reading

Baron, R. and Byrne, D. (1997) *Social Psychology* (8th ed), Needham Heights, Mass: Allyn & Bacon

Bee, H. (1992) *The Developing Child* (6th ed), New York: Harper Collins

Coolican, H. (1995) *Introduction to Research Methods and Statistics in Psychology*, London: Hodder & Stoughton

Deaux, K., Dane, F. & Wrightsman, L. (1993) *Social Psychology in the 90s* (6th ed), Pacific Grove, Calif: Brooks/Cole

Golombok, S. & Fivush, R. (1994) *Gender Development*, Cambridge University Press: Cambridge

Gross, R. (1990) *Key Studies in Psychology*, London: Hodder & Stoughton

Gross, R. (1996) *Psychology: The Science of Mind and Behaviour* (3rd ed), London: Hodder & Stoughton

Gross, R. & McIlveen, R. (1999) *Aspects of Psychology: Memory*, London: Hodder & Stoughton

Hayes, N. (1998) *Foundations of Psychology* (2nd ed), Walton-on-Thames, Middx: Thomas Nelson & Son Ltd.

Hewstone, M., Manstead, A. & Stroebe, W. (1997) *The Blackwell Reader in Social Psychology*, Oxford: Blackwell Publishers

Hill, G. (1998) *Advanced Psychology Through Diagrams*, Oxford: Oxford University Press

Meadows, S. (1993) *The Child as Thinker: The Development and Acquisition of Cognition in Childhood*, London: Routledge

Rutter, M. (1981) *Maternal Deprivation Reassessed* (2nd ed), Harmondsworth, Middx: Penguin

Sabini, J. (1995) *Social Psychology* (2nd ed), New York: W. W. Norton & Co. Inc.

Websites

http://www.bps.org.uk – The British Psychological Society website

http://www.socialpsychology.org/ – general social psychology website

http://www.cityscope.co.uk/nicky/ – Nicky Hayes' website

http://www.ntu.ac.uk/soc/psych/banyard/ – Phil Banyard's website

http://www.gasou.edu/psychweb/psychweb.htm – a general information site recommended by the Association of Teachers of Psychology

http://www.psychol.ucl.ac.uk/ – University of London Department of Psychology; gives a selection of links to psychology-related sites

http://www.psychplace.com/ – general psychology website

http://www.psywww.com/ – large collection of psychology information and resources

http://www.york.ac.uk/inst/ctipsych/ – gateway to academic sites of interest to students and teachers of psychology

http://longman.awl.com/aronson.student/activities/aschconformityexperiment.asp – conformity and obedience

http://www.tsu.umd.edu/dept/psyc/southrl/prism/bill.htm – dealing with conformity and obedience

http://www.altavista.com – a general site; go to the title page 'education' then click on 'psychology'

Index